talk WITH teens

about self and stress

50

Guided Discussions for
School and Counseling Groups

jean sunde peterson

edited by pamela espeland

Free Spirit

PUBLISHING

Library of Congress Cataloging-in-Publication Data
Peterson, Jean Sunde, 1941–
    Talk with teens about self and stress : 50 guided discussions for school and counseling groups / Jean Sunde Peterson : edited by Pamela Espeland.
       p.   cm.
    Includes bibliographical references and index.
    ISBN 0-915793-55-5
    1. Counseling in secondary education—United States.
2. Discussion. 3. Teacher participation in educational counseling—United States. 4. Self-perception in adolescence—United States.
5. Stress in adolescence—United States. I. Espeland, Pamela. II. Title.
LB1620.5.P44 1993
373.14'6—dc20
          93-21514
          CIP

Cover and book design by MacLean and Tuminelly

Cover photograph by David Coates

Index prepared by Eileen Quam and Theresa Wolner

10 9 8 7 6 5 4 3
Printed in the United States of America

The explanation of cults on page 176 is from *The Wrong Way Home* by Arthur J. Deikman. Copyright © 1990 by Arthur J. Deikman. Reprinted by permission of Beacon Press.

Free Spirit Publishing Inc. ·
400 First Avenue North, Suite 616
Minneapolis, MN 55401
(612) 338-2068

dedication

To those who taught me best—
many, many students
in many, many places,
my siblings,
and my children, Sonia and Nathan

acknowledgments

I have been educated by a multitude of individuals in my life. My parents taught me, by example, that teaching is a worthy profession, that service and support of others is important for both self-development and community progress, that meaningful work is an end in itself, and that "process," not "product," is where the fun is. An ongoing liberal arts education, a varied teaching career, and a multilevel life have instructed me further, with a few particular process-oriented mentors, like Joan Ostrander, Ruth Jones, and Loila Hunking, steering me in important directions along the way. My husband, Reuben, continues to provide unwavering support for projects like this one. This is a book about process, not product. It affirms students "in process." It probably also represents my own.

Important in eventually directing me toward gifted education, counseling, and group work with adolescents were school administrators who gave me both rare autonomy and wise advice along the way. They supported experimentation with methodology and content, and they encouraged professional growth. I worked with several fine principals along the way, but I am particularly grateful to two in the Sioux Falls, South Dakota, area: Jack Lauer and Fred Stephens. I also worked under two excellent coordinators of gifted education there, Penny Oldfather and Gail Widman, who provided the same kind of support.

As I became acquainted with students through their writing in my English classes, through extracurriculars, and through foreign language activities, I grew more and more interested in counseling and adolescent psychology. My long friendship with former college roommate, now therapist, Norma McLane Haan had a consulting dimension that became more and more significant as I dealt with complex adolescent issues, particularly during the years discussion groups were basic to the program I directed. She acquainted me with systems theory, taught me wisely as she helped me guide troubled adolescents, and eventually inspired me to continue graduate work in counseling and child development.

Early in my teaching career I began regularly to attend workshops, conferences, and in-service sessions dealing with the affective realm. I took notes, added my thoughts to my files on various topics, consulted with counselors and other mental health professionals, and read books. I am grateful for those experiences and to those who taught me. When I began the discussion groups in Sioux Falls, I had much to draw from. The gifted program I directed there had an ongoing lecture series using medical, business, mental health, and college and university speakers. They, too, educated me. The background information for many of the sessions in this book is based as much on that accumulation of information, ideas, materials, and thoughts as on formal coursework and training.

contents

List of Reproducible Pages viii

introduction   1

About This Book 1
   Description and Benefits 1
   Genesis...1
   Purpose..2
   Assumptions 3

About the Sessions 3
   General Description 3
   Focus 4
   Objectives and Suggestions...4
   Activity Sheets 5
   Background Information 5
   Closure 5
   Sessions for Special Populations..5

Forming a Group 6
   Group Size 6
   Group Composition...6
   Getting Students to Join 7
   How to Approach Students at Risk 7

Assessing Your Readiness to Lead Discussion Groups 8

Guidelines for Group Leaders 9
   General Guidelines 9
   Ethical Behavior 10
   Journal-Writing 10
   Dealing with Students Who Are Quiet or Shy 11
   Counseling Individual Group Members 11
   Handling Emotional Bombshells...11
   Keeping the Topic a Secret 12

Other Uses for These Guided Group Discussions 12
   In the Regular Classroom 12
   To Promote Cohesion in School and Other Groups....................12

a note for parents   13

getting started   14

How to Begin 14
How to Proceed 14
Tips for Group Leaders..15
Endings 16

focus: the self   25

General Background..27
General Objectives 28

the sessions

Personal Strengths and Limitations..29
Three Selves..31
Behind the Facade..33
Does the Stereotype Fit?..36
Going to Extremes 38
Perfectionism 40
Intensity, Compulsivity, and Moderation 44
Learning Styles..47
Who and What Defines Us?..51
Should Test Scores Define Us?..53
Understanding Underachievement 57
Giving Ourselves Permission 63
What's in a Name? 67
Time and Priorities 69
In Control, Out of Control...72
Assessing Self-Esteem 74
Making Mistakes 79
Do Heroes and Heroines Reflect Values? 81
Having Fun...83
Each of Us Is an Interesting Story 86
When We Need Courage 90
A Prisoner of Image 93
Feeling Free 95
Daydreaming...98
Taking Stock 100
A Question of Values: What Matters to Me? 103
Success and Failure 107
Being Alone vs. Being Lonely 109
A Personal Symbol..111

focus: the self and others 113

General Background 115
General Objectives 116

the sessions

How Others See Us 117
Encouragement and Discouragement 120
Those Who Influence 123
Uniquenesses and Similarities 125
Responding to Authority 127
Giving Ourselves Away 132
Best Advice 134
Who Can We Lean On? 136
Gifts We Would Like from People Who Matter..............................138
Getting Our Needs Met...141
Tolerance and Compassion...145

focus: stress 149

General Background 151
General Objectives...152

the sessions

What Is Stress? 153
Sorting Out the Sources of Stress...155
Dealing with Others' Expectations 159
Role Models and Strategies for Coping with Stress.......................163
Is It Harder to Be an Adolescent Today? 165
Taking a Load Off 168
Procrastination 170
Substance Abuse 173
Vulnerability to Cults and Demagogues 175
Centering...177

index 179

about the author 183

list of reproducible pages

Permission for Student Participation 17

Group Guidelines 18

Warm-Up 19

Follow-Up 20

Discussion Group Evaluation 21–23

My Three Selves 32

Underachievers Anonymous 62

Giving Myself Permission 66

My Life Outside of School 71

Rating My Self-Esteem 78

My Story 88–89

Freedom of Choice 97

I Am... 102

A Question of Values 105–106

How Others See Me, How I See Myself 119

Responding to Authority 130–131

My Wish List 140

My Needs 144

Stress Boxes 158

Expectations 162

introduction

about this book

description and benefits

Talk with Teens about Self and Stress was written to meet the need of students to "just talk"—to share their feelings and concerns with supportive peers and an attentive adult. These guided discussions have evolved from many years of working with students, listening to them, and learning about their lives.

Since 1985, I have led approximately 90 groups of students ranging from grades 4 through 12, with many groups involved for a full school term, for a total of over 1,300 sessions. I have also led single-session or short-term groups with adults. The suggestions, activities, and written exercises in this book, along with its flexible-focus format, have been thoroughly tested. You can feel confident about using these materials with your students.

I have witnessed the benefits of these guided discussion groups for students of many ages and ability levels.

- I have seen inspiring results in both well-adjusted students and those at risk. Gifted students have also responded positively to this format.

- I have seen that "just talking" helps to lower stress levels, to normalize "weird" thoughts, and to sort out personal conflict.

- The groups give students who are cynical and negative an experience that makes school "not so bad."

- Students learn to anticipate problems and find support for problem-solving. They feel better about themselves as they become comfortable with others and allow their "real selves" to show during group meetings. The interaction is affirming. In other words, the groups serve a clearly *preventive* function in improving self-esteem and social ease.

- Because the groups involve many students, I have been able to make better use of my own time with regard to student contact.

These are benefits that you will begin noticing and enjoying once your own group is established.

genesis

From 1962 through 1985, I taught English, literature, and language to junior and senior high school students in Iowa, Minnesota, South Dakota, and Berlin, Germany. My years in the classroom tuned me in to the social and emotional worlds of adolescents. When they responded to literature in their journals, when they interacted with me during yearbook meetings, when they worked with me in foreign-language club activities, and when they lingered after class, they told me about themselves.

I learned that they shared many common concerns, but with unique complexities. Most of my students wanted to "be known"—to be more than "just another student," recognized for their individual worth and uniqueness. They readily accepted my invitation to respond personally, in writing, to the literature we were reading in class. In fact, we didn't discuss literature much orally; they wrote in their journals, and I responded in the margins.

There were many reasons for this teaching approach, but three relate to the groups I later developed: I wanted my students to learn to express themselves on paper, I wanted them to become independent thinkers, and I wanted to hear from *everyone* equally, not just from the highly verbal and assertive.

Some students stayed after class to ask advice, to talk about personal pain and growth, or, more frequently, to "just talk." Experiences like these are not uncommon in the teaching world. Students are hungry for acknowledgment and for nonjudgmental listening. I learned that there were many important things they did not discuss with their peers, and they did not always have a comfortable enough relationship with a parent to ask tough questions or express concern and anxiety.

My students, like yours, were fatigued from part-time jobs. They fought with siblings, broke up with sweethearts, and were scared of the future. Many struggled with the hypocrisy of the adults around them and the sad state of the world as they saw it; many responded to these and other issues with sadness and depression. They had a hard time balancing the fragments of their complex lives. Sometimes they felt like exploding from tension. They needed someone to talk to.

In 1985, when I became involved in gifted education, I thought back to the adolescents who had let me know them. I wondered if group discussions, held outside of the regular classroom, might help the high-stress students in the gifted program. I certainly had seen the need for support and attentive listening in the bright students who had attended my classes. I knew that, no matter what their level of capability, they were still adolescents, no more able than anyone else their age to deal with roller-coaster moods, galloping hormones, and conflicts with adults and peers. I decided to offer a group option to deal with social and emotional issues.

The groups did not catch on immediately, but by the second semester there were three, with ten to twelve students each. The next year there were six groups, then ten, with two groups per day coordinated with the noon lunch schedule. Eventually administrators, counselors, student teachers, and guests from other districts came to watch, and almost invariably they would remark, "It's too bad *all* students can't have this opportunity." I agreed wholeheartedly. Observers also commented that they never would have suspected that students had so much to deal with behind their cool facades.

The students were faithful in attending the group meetings in spite of the fact that attendance was voluntary, though strongly encouraged. The groups became close through steady, undramatic weekly contact, and when there was a crisis, whether personal or institutional, there was a ready support system. The students taught me, they taught each other, and they learned about themselves. The topics were not necessarily "heavy," but the students responded to them, relaxing and "just talking."

I eventually wrote manuals for the groups and shared them. *Talk with Teens* grew out of those manuals, their content tempered and shaped by years of experience.

purpose

The purpose of these guided discussion groups is to serve the affective needs of adolescent students. Through the groups, students gain self-awareness, and that in turn helps them to make better decisions, solve problems, and deal more effectively with their various environments. They learn to affirm themselves in all of their complexity, and they feel more in control of their lives.

It may be enough to say that the purpose of these groups is simply to let students express themselves—to "just talk." They need practice putting words on their feelings and concerns. As much as some of them talk socially, they may not be skilled at communicating their feelings honestly and with clarity. Later in life, their relationships and their employment will all be enhanced if they are able to talk about what is important to them. Adolescence is a good time to learn those skills.

- A group can provide a noncompetitive environment where no grades are given and where everyone is fairly equal.

- In the affective realm, students have much in common. Everyone is navigating the uneven seas of adolescence, with complex feelings, frustrations, and anxieties, and without the skills to ensure smooth sailing. Discussion groups can provide a place for safe talk about this journey.

According to the feedback students have given me for many years, the topics covered here are often not discussed, even among best friends.* In end-of-the-year written assessments, students have told me

* Topics *not* covered here include AIDS and other sexually transmitted diseases, sexual and other physical abuse, teenage pregnancy, substance abuse, steroid use, and health and nutrition. It is assumed (I hope correctly) that these topics are covered elsewhere in the school curriculum, perhaps in health, family living, or other courses. A few sessions may mention or briefly focus on some of these issues, but only to provide students with an opportunity to practice articulating their feelings and concerns about them.

that they are grateful for having received guidance in important areas of their lives—and for having been "forced" to deal with these topics in a safe, supportive environment.

Students inevitably gain social skills through group interaction. Often, social discomfort contributes to, and is exacerbated by, poor functioning in school. Learning about what they and others have in common, learning to listen, gaining experience in initiating and responding socially, and becoming aware of how they are seen by others promotes social ease and enhances self-esteem, both of which can help to make school a more pleasant place.

The format of *Talk with Teens* is not designed specifically and formally to teach group skills or to acquaint students with the vocabulary of group process. However, many such skills and some helpful terminology will likely be learned along the way. Guided group discussion is a process-more-than-product activity, yet ultimately it aims to enhance the skills of articulating social and emotional concerns. The focus, the objectives, and the suggestions for content and closure contained in each session should give you enough of a framework that your students will have good, solid, invigorating experiences.

It is important to understand that the purpose of these groups is not to "fix" students. Even though the questions are designed to provoke a healthy level of introspection, the emphasis is always on the experience of articulating feelings and thoughts in the presence of others who listen and care. These are not meant to be therapy groups. Of course, some noticeable changes in attitude and behavior may occur, but even when it may appear that these are brought about by the response and support of the group, other factors such as changes at home, the healing effect of time, or developmental "leaps" may also have contributed. A group might simply help to *sustain* a student through a difficult year.

As is the case whenever adults stand firmly beside adolescents for a time, establish trust, and participate in their complex lives, you will serve your students best by hearing them well and offering support as they find their own direction.

assumptions

The format and content of *Talk with Teens* reflect the following assumptions, which you may want to keep in mind as you lead your own group.

1. All students have a desire to be heard, listened to, taken seriously, and respected.

2. Some students who are quiet, shy, intimidated, or untrusting will not spontaneously offer comments, but they, too, want to be recognized and understood as unique individuals.

3. All students need support, no matter how strong and successful they might seem.

4. All students feel stressed at times. Some feel stressed most or even all of the time.

5. All adolescents are sensitive to family tension. Some are trying hard to keep their families afloat or intact. They may be unaware of how much they are using bad behavior to keep their parents focused on them—and together.

6. All adolescents feel angry at times.

7. All adolescents feel socially inept and uncomfortable at times.

8. All adolescents worry about the future at times.

9. All adolescents, no matter how smooth and self-confident they may appear, need practice talking honestly about feelings.

10. Everyone wears a facade at times.

about the sessions
general description

The guided discussion sessions in *Talk with Teens* are appropriate for:

- the general population
- a number of special populations
- any adolescent age level, with possible adjustments in vocabulary, session length, and content for younger age groups and for some ability levels.

The vocabulary used in explanatory material is appropriate for teachers and counselors. In the written exercises, it is geared "up" rather than "down," since it is generally easier to make adjustments for younger children than in the other direction. Older adolescents, especially those with high ability, respond better to language that challenges rather than patronizes.

For some junior high/middle school groups, some written exercises may need to be shortened and some vocabulary changed. Some of the suggestions might not fit, depending on the setting and the group's intellectual level. Some of the sessions assume a high abstract-reasoning ability, and some deal with issues that are suitable only for mature students. You will need to assess the individual sessions to determine which ones might be most helpful, enjoyable, and appropriate for your group. Be sure not to underestimate your students' awareness of the world just because they are chronologically young. At the same time, you will need to consider developmental realities and community sensitivities.

Special populations who might benefit from these guided group discussions include:

- students at risk for dropping out
- students with behavior problems
- students who are "down" or depressed
- students having difficulty with adult authority
- teenage parents
- underachievers
- students who have been labeled "gifted"
- students in, or returning from, treatment for substance abuse or eating disorders
- students in transition during family changes.

Sessions are arranged in a purposeful progression, but may be rearranged to create a short-term program or to become part of a particular agenda.

focus

Why have a focus for each session? All students are not as flexible as they might seem, even if they appear to be quite "unstructured." On the other hand, some are quite flexible, and, especially if they are verbal and spontaneous, they may prefer a loose format. They might say, "Just let us come in here and hang out. We'll find something to talk about." However, many are in the other camp, and they quickly tire of "not really doing anything."

Students who are more orderly and structured like to know that time spent in a group is worthwhile in more specific terms than just "feeling good." Lacking a focus, if the group is a voluntary activity, they will choose not to come when something else is more inviting or pressing. They might also object to

the fact that assertive members set the pace and topic each time. Students with new and dramatic needs each week can quickly dominate, and others will either defer and listen or leave, frustrated that their issues are not being addressed. Discussion groups should not be just for natural talkers.

On the other hand, group discussions need not be rigidly programmed. Although *Talk with Teens* proposes a focus for each session, with several sessions building on a theme, there is great potential for nimbly changing direction during discussion. A good leader can accommodate various strands that need to be pursued, yet still gently steer the group to closure, acknowledging perhaps that the focus inspired unexpected directions. Especially with topics students may perceive as intimidating and difficult, the focus is an excuse to persist with tough questions and deal with issues and problems, not just gripes and frustrations.

Also, having a focus makes it easy for you to communicate with administrators, parents, and other faculty about your group and what you do together. Many outsiders assume that discussion groups are for teacher-bashing, for airing family secrets, or for rewarding good students, as if the meetings were some kind of elitist "dessert." Being able to say "We've been dealing with stress for the past four weeks," or "We're focusing on self-awareness this semester," or, more specifically, "We've been talking about perfectionism" helps to lessen any such anxiety and also underscores that your group is dealing with substantial issues.

objectives and suggestions

The objectives listed for each session tell you what to work toward and what to expect if the general suggestions are followed. They may also be useful in communicating content to administrators, parents, and teachers who wonder what your group is doing. You may want to prepare a list of objectives for parent conferences, for example. The objectives are not meant to be read to the students.

The suggestions are just that—suggestions. Use all, some, or none of them, and adapt those you use to meet the needs of your group. Time limits and group temperament are two of many factors you will want to consider when choosing which suggestions and activities to pursue.

activity sheets

Several of the sessions include activity sheets that may be photocopied for group use. In my experience, these written exercises do not make discussions too structured, and most students do not resist them. It all depends on how they are used.

Especially when they are not used too often, students actually *appreciate* the handouts for giving them an opportunity to think quietly and focus at the outset of a meeting; to write, objectify, and perhaps edit their thoughts; and to sort and ponder complex issues. Everyone has a chance to be heard. Shy members can share without having to compete with assertive folks. Discussion can involve only a few or all of the questions or items, and the students can be polled for categories of responses or asked for specific answers.

You may want to keep file folders for all group members and have them leave their activity sheets in their folders at the close of each session. This will ensure that sensitive handouts don't end up on the classroom floor or circulating through the halls, with personal thoughts revealed indiscreetly through carelessness. Tell group members that they can decide what to do with their activity sheets when the group experience comes to an end.

background information

For many of the sessions, a few paragraphs of background information are provided at the beginning. Like the objectives, the background is not meant to be read to the students. It is designed to help you prepare for the session and think broadly about the topic at hand; to offer some basic information about the topic that might be useful to you during the session; to inspire further reading; to encourage you to anticipate student concerns; and to assist you in determining a possible direction for the discussion, according to the needs of your group.

This work is a synthesis of several years' worth of information gleaned from seminars, workshops, in-service training, lectures, course work, consultation with experts, and my own experience interacting with adolescents at all levels in my teaching and counseling careers. Whenever I need important information, I try to get to the best sources I can find. The background information contains some of what I have accumulated.

closure

Each session includes a suggestion for closure. It is always a good idea to end a session with some kind of summary or tying-up activity, whether you provide it yourself or offer your students the opportunity. Inherent in closure is the reminder that their discussions are purposeful, that they share common concerns, and that they have been heard. If an important new thought is introduced in the closing minutes, it is still good to have some kind of deliberate closure, even if it includes suggesting that the group continue with the new strand next time.

sessions for special populations

- Students experiencing family transitions can benefit from the sessions in the Focus: Stress section. They might also find affirmation and be able to express sad feelings in the sessions "Personal Strengths and Limitations," "Who and What Defines Us?", "Each of Us Is an Interesting Story," "Taking Stock," and "A Personal Symbol."

- Students at risk might benefit from the sessions "Does the Stereotype Fit?", "Learning Styles," "Who and What Defines Us?", "Should Test Scores Define Us?", "Understanding Underachievement," "In Control, Out of Control," "A Prisoner of Image," "Feeling Free," "Encouragement and Discouragement," "Those Who Influence," "Responding to Authority," "Gifts We Would Like from People Who Matter," and "Getting Our Needs Met."

- Students who are feeling down or depressed often find some of the sessions geared to the gifted and the sessions in the Focus: Stress section to be helpful. In addition, the following sessions can be valuable: "Three Selves," "Behind the Facade," "In Control, Out of Control," "Assessing Self-Esteem," "Having Fun," "When We Need Courage," "Being Alone vs. Being Lonely," "Giving Ourselves Away," "Gifts We Would Like from People Who Matter," and "Getting Our Needs Met." Teenage parents and students returning from, or currently in, treatment for substance abuse or eating disorders might also find these sessions helpful.

- *All* sessions are relevant to students of high ability. Several sessions are especially suited to gifted students, whether high achievers or underachievers: "Perfectionism," "Intensity, Compulsivity, and Moderation," "Understanding Underachievement," "Giving Ourselves Permission," and "Dealing with Others' Expectations." Most of these also generate good discussion with students at risk who have high capability.

forming a group
group size

In my experience, ideal group size varies according to age level. For high school students, between eight and twelve is optimum. With more than twelve it is difficult to hear from everyone adequately on any subject, especially when using an activity sheet. With fewer than eight, there is less opportunity for variety in input, and there is a possibility that familiarity will interfere with seriousness of purpose.

For junior high/middle school students, a group size of six to eight seems to work best. Class periods are shorter, and students need more time and individual attention to articulate their thoughts and attain depth.

group composition

I have found that the best groups are often those where students do not know each other well outside the group. They seem to feel more free to share, and they do not have to preface all comments with "Well, someone in here has heard me say this before, but...." On the other hand, I have also had good groups where most of the students knew each other well. The groups helped them know each other *better.*

Depending on the size of the student population you will draw from, you may not have a choice. If the students in your group know each other, it is important to move the group beyond the natural division of "friends" and "non-friends." Having a focus, with specific activities and written exercises, helps to ensure that the "friends group" does not dominate or antagonize the others with inside humor. Encouraging them to change seating each time can also be helpful.

I like to promote the idea of using the groups to break down barriers. For general discussion groups, I tend to prefer a 50/50 split with achievers and under-

achievers, at-risk and not at-risk, highly involved and not-so-involved. Otherwise, each continues to stereotype the other, with the "in" or successful students feeling no common ground with the disenfranchised or low-achieving students, and vice versa.

If several groups are being formed at one time, this split can be accomplished by initially compiling a list of all students who accept the invitation to participate and then "sorting" the list. Of course, recruitment will have to target those less likely to feel welcome. In some cases, the highest-functioning students may be the most reluctant to join, fearing that the groups are geared only to "problems" and that participation will somehow stigmatize them. Students at risk and underachieving students may think that they are the only ones with stresses, vulnerabilities, and fears. All groups have a great deal to learn from each other, and the group setting can be an ideal learning environment.

Gifted students are often not comfortable talking in intellectually heterogeneous groups. Many of their problems and concerns may be similar to those of other students, but usually they share more willingly and easily when others of similar intellect are there to hear them and can express their own concerns at a similarly complex level. A mixture of various levels of *achievement*, not *ability*, can make highly productive discussion groups for gifted students. Often, underachievers are amazed that achievers have social and emotional problems; some achievers are equally amazed that underachievers can be highly intelligent. Provoking that discovery of common ground is a good place to start.

If mixing is not possible in your setting, or if your group is homogeneous regarding an area of concern and has a specific purpose and agenda, you can still use these guided discussions with confidence, since they deal with common adolescent issues.

Mixing genders is also good, even though it is not always possible and might not be advantageous or appropriate for certain topics. However, it is important for males and females to learn about each other in a safe and honest environment, outside of the regular classroom and apart from usual social settings. It is also important for students of both genders to learn how to communicate with, and in the presence of, each other.

Especially for students who are shy or who have little social experience, a discussion group can provide a chance to have contact with the other gender. But even for the highly social, a group can raise awareness of gender issues and enhance the students' ability to function effectively with each other in social relationships now and in the future, in employment, and perhaps in the board room someday.

On the other hand, same-gender grouping also has advantages and is particularly appropriate when the issues are gender-specific, especially troublesome and gender-related, or perceived to be unsafe for discussion with members of the other gender. The age of the group members might be a determining factor in regard to the last aspect. Same-gender groups can sometimes empower students in ways that mixed groups cannot. Homogeneity may be especially desirable in a first-stage recovery group, for example. Obviously, decisions about grouping must be based on the goals and purpose of the group.

Because the sessions are mostly geared to the social and emotional, not to the intellectual or academic, it is best to try for homogeneity regarding age. High school juniors and seniors are a lot alike, but most seniors are looking ahead more intensely. Sophomore issues are usually different from junior issues, and even seventh and eighth graders often have a difficult time connecting with each other about social and emotional concerns. Relationship and separation issues differ along the age continuum, and it is best when students can communicate with others in their own age group.

Granted, boys and girls may differ greatly in physical and emotional maturity, particularly in junior high/middle school. Still, a less mature boy can gain from hearing about the concerns of the girls he is around daily, and maybe even vice versa.

getting students to join

The best way to get students to join your group is to invite them personally. In any event, I recommend that you *not* call it a "counseling group" when describing it to prospective group members. Some students are automatically turned off and turned away by that label. Later on, should someone ask if, in fact, it is a counseling group, you might explain that "counseling" basically means "talking and listening" with someone trained in the process, and, in that regard, your group could be called a counseling group. However, for recruitment purposes, "discussion group" is both accurate and more appealing. It carries no negative stigma.

"Support group" is appropriate when there is a common, specific agenda, or a shared problem area. If the group is largely preventive, with self-awareness and personal growth as goals, then "support" can sound too problem-oriented for many students. In any case, "discussion group" is my preference.

I have contacted students individually to explain a proposed group, and I have called in small groups and full-size discussion groups to hear the plan. In either case, you will want to assure the students that joining the group is not a dangerous thing to do. The advantage of calling in the group as a whole is that the students can see who else will be attending. On the other hand, some might decide against joining for that very reason, without giving the group a chance. When meeting with students individually, it is good to give them the names of a few prospective members—if they ask, and if it is possible to share names in advance.

Be sure to emphasize the social, as well as the emotional, purposes of the group. Students respond well to the idea of getting to know new people and learning to know current acquaintances and friends in new ways. They also can relate to the idea of talking about adolescent stress. Explain that, beyond pursuing general goals, the group will help to determine its own unique direction. That much of an explanation usually suffices. If students want to know more, show them the table of contents for *Talk with Teens*. The session titles are varied, and students usually find them interesting—and unexpected.

Especially for high school students, it helps to tell them that once you get to know them better through the group experience, you will be able to write more complete and accurate job, college, or scholarship recommendations for them when they are needed. Explain that you will also be a better and more informed advocate for them if they ever need assistance.

how to approach students at risk

If your group is to serve students at risk, there will probably be school or district guidelines for identifying prospective group members. Identifying factors might include:

- family disruption
- substance abuse
- physical or sexual abuse

- family tragedy
- lack of family support for school attendance or achievement
- a potential for dropping out of school.

Some students at risk might be eager to join a group, but many probably will not be. If attendance is voluntary, meet with the students individually and privately. Explain that you will be leading a discussion group for students who are dealing with stress, and you are inviting them to participate. If the student is a rebel, someone who is anti-authority, an under-achieving student with high ability, or a "joker," state that you are looking for interesting, complex students who can help to make a good group. Say that you are looking specifically for students who express their abilities in unusual ways because you don't want a group that is afraid to challenge and think, or students who always do just what is expected of them. Reframing characteristics usually considered "troublesome" in this way often takes students by surprise and encourages them to participate.

However, no matter what a particular student's behavior might be, always present the group's purpose honestly: to give students a chance to "just talk" about issues that are important to all adolescents. Be sincere, accepting, and supportive in your invitation. With students at risk, as with all prospective group members, take care not to frighten them away by sounding too invasive or personal. Give them time to warm up to the idea of interacting with others about personal issues.

assessing your readiness to lead discussion groups

If you are not used to dealing with groups of students in an informal discussion setting, you may find it helpful to keep the following suggestions and observations in mind.

- If group members have high ability levels, recognize that some, or many, may be more intellectually nimble than you are. On the other hand, some may be less nimble, and you will need to be patient.

- If you are careful to stick to social and emotional issues, there will be little opportunity for students to play competitive, "one-up" verbal games, especially since these issues are less likely to be debatable.

- For most students, the affective dimension involves more personal risk-taking than the academic. Social and emotional areas are much less "controllable" than the intellectual realm.

- Significant people in their lives might have focused more on academic than on affective needs. Some students will be eager and immediately grateful for the emphasis on the social and emotional; some might be uncomfortable or skeptical at first; some might even be frightened by it. Whatever the response, your concentrated attention on the affective will probably be a new experience for them.

You might also want to consider your own motives for establishing groups for students, as well as your sense of security around all kinds of students. Ask yourself these questions:

- Can you avoid feeling competitive with them, or needing to assert control over them?

- Can you not be threatened by them? Remember, you have longer life experience.

- Can you stay focused on their social and emotional issues?

- Can you deal with them simply as human beings with frailties, insecurities, sensitivities, and vulnerabilities, regardless of their achievements (or lack of achievement)?

- Can you avoid needing to "put them in their place"?

- Can you accept their defenses, such as arrogance or rebelliousness, at the outset, and give them time to let themselves be vulnerable?

- Can you recognize that they may not be accomplished risk-takers socially, academically, and/or emotionally, and that they might need to be encouraged to take appropriate risks?

- Can you look honestly at some of your own stereotypes or negative feelings that might interfere in your work with various student populations, and can you put them aside for the duration of the group experience?

- Can you let them teach you about themselves?

If you can answer "yes" to all or most of these questions, don't worry—you're more than ready to take on a roomful of students.

guidelines for group leaders

general guidelines

The following general guidelines are designed to help you lead successful and meaningful discussion groups. You may want to review them from time to time over the life of a group.

1. Be prepared to learn how to lead a group by *doing it.* Let the students know that this is your attitude. If you are not a trained counselor, ask a school counselor for information on group process and counseling techniques. You might also arrange to co-facilitate your first group with a counselor or trained group leader. Even if you lead groups regularly, an occasional refresher on group process is a good idea.

2. Don't think that you have to be an expert on every topic covered. Tell the students at the outset that you want to learn *with them* and *from them.* That is a wonderful place to start, and your students will respond. For most sessions, having all of the right information is not the key to success. Trust your adult wisdom; it will serve you well. That's one thing you have that your students don't.

3. Monitor group interaction and work toward contribution from everyone without making that an issue. Remember that shy students can gain a great deal just by listening. Of course, you will want to encourage everyone to participate, but never insist. The written exercises and activity sheets can be used to provide quiet students with a comfortable opening for sharing.

4. Keep the session focus in mind, but be flexible about direction. Your group may lead you in new directions that are as worthwhile as the stated focus and suggestions.

5. It is probably best to go into each session with two sessions in mind, since the one you have planned may not get as much response as expected. You can always unobtrusively guide the group in a new direction. Try several approaches to a topic before dropping it, however. It might simply require some "baking time."

6. Be *willing* to role model everything, even though it may not always be *necessary* for promoting group interaction. (See page 15, tip #9, for cautionary statements in this regard.) We all benefit from positive role models, and if you aren't willing to self-disclose, your students may wonder why they should be expected to reveal their thoughts and feelings.

7. Every now and then, check out how the students are feeling about the group process. Is there anything they would like to do differently or change? Are they comfortable sharing their feelings and concerns? What has been helpful? Have they noticed any problems that need addressing, such as discussions being dominated by a few, not enough flexibility in direction, a personality conflict within the group, or too much leader direction? This "processing" provides an opportunity for students to practice tact in addressing group issues. Ask for suggestions and incorporate those that fit the overall purpose of the group. Be aware that some students may press for "no focus" for a long time. You may want to review the rationale for focus outlined on page 4 above. Depending on the makeup of your group, you may choose to delay questions about format until the benefits have become fairly clear. Or simply be prepared to explain the purpose of the format while emphasizing the "flexible" part. Support the group and give guidance as they make progress in overcoming group problems.

8. If group energy consistently or increasingly lags, discuss that in group. Let the students help you figure out how to energize the discussions and/or deal with group inhibitions. However, do not readily reject the idea of maintaining a focus for each session. Perhaps you need to check out your questioning style or more deftly follow some strands that come up spontaneously. Or perhaps you need to be more selective in choosing your topics. The written exercises and activity sheets can help to encourage sharing.

ethical behavior

Your ethical behavior as group leader is of utmost importance. Sharing confidential group information in the teachers' lounge, with parents, or in the community will not only be hurtful, but may also ultimately destroy the possibility of any group activity in your school. Trust is quickly lost, and it is difficult or even impossible to reestablish.

If you plan to conduct groups in a school setting, but are unfamiliar with ethical guidelines for counselors, get a copy of such guidelines from your school counselor and read it thoroughly. Be especially aware of your responsibilities regarding confidentiality. This includes familiarizing yourself with situations in which confidentiality may be waived, such as when abuse is suspected, when someone is in danger or may be a danger to others, or when there is a court order. The "informed consent" aspect can be addressed by discussing format, content, confidentiality, and purpose when extending the invitation to attend the group, or at the first meeting.

You may wish to address these issues in a letter to parents asking their permission for their children to attend the group. For a sample letter (which you may modify to include these issues), see page 17. Please note that this letter is intended for groups not designed for specific problem areas, and feel free to adapt it accordingly.

journal-writing

Depending on the purpose of your group, whether it is mandatory or voluntary, what other responsibilities group members have, and the level of access group members will have to you outside of group meetings, you might consider inviting them to do some journal-writing. Keep the following points in mind as you extend the invitation.

- Groups that serve special populations, and are perhaps more consciously therapeutic, can benefit greatly from journal-writing and leader feedback.

- Journal-writing can add a valuable dimension to any group experience. When students have the opportunity to put their thoughts in writing, this often helps them to articulate, clarify, expand on, and sort ideas and issues that are important to them. They are more likely to remember ideas and issues they want to bring up in group, and they feel more confident about expressing them.

- An important goal of the group experience is learning to articulate thoughts and feelings in order to enhance relationships with friends, parents, and boyfriends/girlfriends now, and with co-workers, college roommates, marriage partners, and/or children in the future. Journal-writing—with encouragement from you to share in group some of the gist or specifics of what they write—can aid in this learning process. Some group members who are not assertive may express themselves more comfortably on paper.

- Some adolescents eagerly write their feelings, a fact that is obvious in the sometimes voluminous notes that are passed in junior and senior high schools. Others see writing as a burdensome chore. Sometimes this reflects a negative experience with writing in the classroom. Reassure the group that their journal-writing will not be graded. They will not have to worry about punctuation, spelling, sentence structure, or any of the other mechanics of writing. What is important is what they have to say, not how they choose to say it.

- Some students have a strong aversion to writing, perhaps because they prefer another mode of creative expression. Visual artists, musicians, and kinesthetic learners sometimes find it difficult to write—or to sustain writing. You might encourage those students to use their journals as "sketchbooks" or as idea "scrapbooks." They may draw or doodle, include poems or scripts, create cartoons with captions—anything they choose, as long as their efforts communicate their feelings.

- In schools where there is considerable journal-writing in language arts classes, students are less likely to welcome journals in the discussion groups. There can definitely be "journal burnout." Be sensitive to this issue while explaining that journal-writing during the group experience will probably be very different from journal-writing in their regular classes. Rather than writing about specific topics, they will have the chance to explore their feelings and issues that really matter to them.

- Students often need strong enticement to join groups, especially when groups are first being established. They are most receptive when the group experience does not seem like "work."

Journal-writing can easily be perceived as an "assignment" or "work"—"more of the same"—and turn students off. Explain that it is always simply an option if, in fact, it is not mandatory. "Sell" it as an opportunity rather than an assignment. Encourage reluctant writers to give it a try.

- Invite all journal-writers to share their journals with you, if they choose. This can give your students a chance to communicate privately with you about important concerns that cannot be comfortably discussed in the group. When my students have shared their journals with me, I have responded in writing in the margins. This is a good way to carry on a "dialogue" with students who may not feel comfortable sharing their thoughts and feelings orally within the group. It gives everyone a chance for one-on-one communication with the group leader; conscientious feedback is appreciated and essential. However, journals should not take the place of "just talking." Remind reluctant talkers that while you are willing to read their journals, and you appreciate their confidence in sharing them with you, it is also important for them to contribute to the group.

dealing with students who are quiet or shy

Earnest efforts to ask students who are quiet or shy for at least one or two comments each meeting can help them to feel included and gradually increase their courage or willingness to share. Although listening can be as valuable as speaking in finding commonalities and gaining self-awareness, it is important for reticent students to be heard by their peers, if only at modest levels. Even small talk between a leader and a shy student while everyone is getting settled contributes to comfort and ease, which eventually might help to generate spontaneous comments.

The value of communication with peers, in contrast to communication with the leader, should not be underestimated. Post-group feedback has indicated that quiet students gain as much or more than assertive students from the group experience. The fact that the dominant American culture values extroversion and assertiveness often makes natural reticence seem odd. Groups can actually help to affirm quiet personal styles. Perhaps a lack of sharing with peers prior to, and outside of, the group experience has left quiet students feeling poorly informed and "on the outside." Just listening to other group members can be valuable. Using the activity sheets gives everyone, including shy students, a chance to receive the attention of the group and be heard.

counseling individual group members

I have found that when a level of trust has been established in the group and between students and leader, individuals with pressing needs will seek out the leader outside of the group. That assumes, of course, that the leader is accessible.

If you will not be on the premises every day, it is important to make an announcement in the group about times when you will be available. If you have created an atmosphere that is safe for communication with peers, your students will likely trust you to be there in times of crisis or for special concerns. As in everything, moderation is the key. Too much emphasis at group sessions on outside conferencing can turn off students who do not want to connect the groups to "counseling."

handling emotional bombshells

Most students are appropriately discreet in what they share in group, especially when the leader does not pry or *need* to know private information. However, you can probably expect some highly charged moments to occur along the way, most often because someone suddenly shares what may be an "emotional bombshell."

What happens when something shocking comes out, when someone breaks down and cries, or when intense conflict arises within the group? No one can predict these events with any accuracy, of course, since every group has its own unique dynamics, and groups by nature are full of surprises. However, you can learn to trust your instincts. With time and experience, you will be able to anticipate—and perhaps avert—many crisis situations. If they occur, you can be prepared.

Have tissues handy for the student who cries, but affirm the emotion in your facial expression and body language and accept the tears as real and valid. When appropriate, ask the student what, if anything, he or she would like from the group. Verbal or nonverbal support? A hug? Or would the student like for the group just to listen?

If a student makes a dramatic revelation, immediately remind the group about the importance of confidentiality. You might say, "It probably took courage for _____ (name of student) to share that. It wasn't easy. She/he trusted you as a group. Remember—what comes out in the group stays in the group. If you are tempted to share this with someone outside the group, bite your tongue. That's *very* important. We want to protect our group." Beware of exaggerated responses, both nonverbal and verbal, which can reinforce the idea that a particular revelation is "too much to handle." The sharer might, in fact, have been "testing" that belief.

You may need to consult with a school counselor or administrator to learn what to do in specific situations. For example, if a student drops an "emotional bombshell" about abuse or suicide, you will want to know how to follow up. Your district likely has guidelines specific to these issues. It is best to know them ahead of time.

Groups are ideal settings for practicing conflict resolution. Help those in disagreement to talk it out. You might also pursue helpful material on conflict resolution in your school library, or ask your school counselor for strategies your group might use to deal with dissension. Be aware of your own possible resistance to dealing with conflict. Your own fears might prevent your students from handling the situation in a healthy manner.

keeping the topic a secret

If your group is voluntary and a session topic is announced in advance, some students may elect not to come if the topic doesn't immediately sound interesting or personally applicable to them. You want group attendance to be consistent; it is distracting and damaging when ten students show up one week and only two the next. Therefore, I recommend that you use a "trust me" response when students ask about the next session's topic. Suggest that they show up and be surprised. Remind them that one can never anticipate the interesting directions a particular topic might take. Besides, many topics are more complex than they first appear.

other uses for these guided group discussions

in the regular classroom

Talk with Teens can also be useful in the regular classroom. Weekly discussions, or a limited daily series of units, can be part of the curriculum in health, home economics, life skills, social science, or language arts, among several possibilities. Discussion is particularly meaningful for students when it deals with the self. Class periods spent in home room, when designed to enhance self-esteem and create positive interaction in a school, can use these sessions effectively if the time allowed is adequate.

Group dynamics differ, of course, depending on whether a particular class has thirty students or ten, but the focus and most of the strategies work with both. Since a discussion of an activity sheet can easily take an hour with a group of ten, adjustments must be made when activity sheets are used with larger groups. Classes can be divided into small groups for sharing, for example.

to promote cohesion in school and other groups

Selected sessions can be used effectively to promote group cohesion in athletic and academic teams, in music groups, and in school clubs. They may also serve the same purpose in church and community groups. Some, such as "Learning Styles," "Giving Ourselves Permission," and "Uniquenesses and Similarities," with slight adaptations, have been used at choral retreats, Governor's Schools, women's conferences and retreats, and staff development sessions.

a note for parents

Talk with Teens about Self and Stress can be a valuable tool for getting to know your adolescents. It can help you to access what they are thinking and feeling; the issues that are important to them; their problems, hopes and plans for the future.

You may have noticed that parents and teenagers often have difficulty sustaining conversations (yes, probably an understatement). Sometimes it's hard to know what to talk about besides schoolwork and headphones. Parents often don't know what subjects are "safe" and what subjects are "taboo." Sometimes *all* subjects seem to be "off limits."

Students may say to someone outside the family, "There are just some things I'm not comfortable telling them—or asking them." Teenage sons and daughters tend to be moody, becoming more and more reticent and private at home. *Talk with Teens* can give you a way to break down some barriers that have gone up since your children entered the teenage years.

Scan the background information and suggestions for possible topics and conversation-starters. They will also provide you with insights into developmental issues that both you and your children may be wrestling with. Parents often forget what adolescence felt like, and the information in the sessions can help to remind you of the complexities involved.

Most of the sessions in *Talk with Teens*—especially those in the sections titled Focus: The Self and Focus: The Self and Others—can serve as catalysts for family discussion. Many students over the years have taken the activity sheets home for their parents to fill out, especially the ones for the sessions "Learning Styles," "Giving Ourselves Permission," "Each of Us Is an Interesting Story," "Uniquenesses and Similarities," and "Getting Our Needs Met." Most personal issues, such as perfectionism, dealing with authority, "learning," and image, remain with us as adults and are good to discuss even with young adolescents, who are beginning to be aware that these are their issues, too. The other Self topics can also provoke important self-disclosure in us as parents. Such sharing can be helpful to adolescents in pursuit of their own identity.

Several of the sessions in the section titled Focus: Stress are also worth discussing as a family. Expectations, coping strategies, procrastination, and sources of stress are particularly good subjects for family sharing. We are never "done" with such concerns in our lives, and it is good to admit our humanness to our growing children. Such non-authoritarian "realness" can help to create dialogue.

getting started

how to begin

Begin the first meeting by letting the students know how pleased and excited you are that they will be part of the group. Remind them that the purpose of the group is to "just talk"—to share their feelings and concerns with each other and with you, and to offer and accept support.

Be sure to explain that, during group meetings, you will not be a "teacher" in the usual sense of the word. Instead, the focus will be on them. You will be their guide, listening carefully, sharing your own experiences and insights when appropriate, and helping them to connect with each other. Emphasize that you will all learn from each other.

Move next to introductions and a get-acquainted activity, such as the Warm-Up on page 19. Tell the students to silently and slowly read through all of the sentence beginnings; this will help them to formulate entire thoughts rather than one-word answers. Then invite responses. Or, if you prefer, go directly to the session you have chosen to start the group.

At some point during your first meeting, distribute copies of the Group Guidelines on page 18. Go over them one at a time. Read them aloud or ask for volunteers to read them. Ask if anyone has questions, or if there is anything they don't understand. Tell the students that everyone is expected to follow these guidelines for as long as the group exists—including you. Explain that although they may not know how to do all of these things and behave in all of these ways right now, they will be learning and practicing these skills over the life of the group.

how to proceed

First-year groups, particularly at younger ages, often need more structure than more experienced groups. It also takes a while to establish ease and fluidity in discussion, especially when students are not acquainted outside of the group. At experienced levels, students are able to deal with more abstract and personal topics with little introduction, and they are likely to be more patient and tolerant regarding experimentation with format. First-year groups of older students usually attain depth more quickly than younger groups, although the presence of even one or two spontaneous, honest middle schoolers can move a young group quickly into significant interaction.

Follow the suggestions in each session description for introducing the topic, for generating discussion, and for managing the written activities. You will probably find many more suggestions than you will need for a session. Teachers and counselors who used my original manuals told me that they appreciated having several suggestions from which to choose, and that is why I have included many here.

You may find it difficult to follow the printed text of *Talk with Teens* while leading the discussions. Rather than reading anything word-for-word to your group, it is best to familiarize yourself thoroughly with the content of a session before meeting with the students. Then you will have in mind a general direction and some ideas for pursuing various discussion strands, while keeping an eye on the session materials.

Sometimes your group may generate a good discussion for the entire session on only the first suggestion. This is to be expected, and there is nothing wrong with that. The more flexible you can be, the better. Never feel that you need to finish everything I have suggested.

Be aware that even when students enjoy the group, they can forget to come to meetings. If your group is voluntary, you may need to remind the students for several weeks about meeting times and places. Eventually attendance will become a habit.

tips for group leaders

1. Remind the students that anything said in the group stays in the group. Confidentiality is especially important when sensitive information is shared.

2. Ask open-ended questions, not "yes" and "no" questions, to generate discussion. "How . . . ," "What . . . ," "When . . . ," and "Where . . . " are preferable to "Do . . . " and "Did . . . " for asking questions. For reluctant students, closed questions such as "Was it a sad time?" offer low risk.

3. Respond with "Tell us more about . . . ," "Put words on that feeling . . . ," "Help us understand . . . ," "Can you give an example of . . . ," or "What do you mean by . . . ."

4. Always allow students to pass if they prefer not to speak. This applies to any group activity, including questionnaires, checklists, and group discussions. Make it clear from the beginning that nobody ever *has to* speak, even though you hope you can get to know *all* of them through the discussions.

5. Don't preach. Your students probably hear enough of that already. This experience should be different.

6. Don't judge. Let your students "just talk," and accept what they say.

7. Take them seriously and validate their feelings. For some group members, this might be a rare or entirely new experience. Paraphrasing ("You felt she didn't understand"), checking ("Did I hear

you correctly?"), asking for more information ("I don't think I quite understand..."), acknowledging feelings ("I can see how upset that made you"), or simply offering an "Mmmmm" in response to a comment shows that you are listening and want to understand.

8. Relax and let the group be more about process than product. It may not always be apparent that something specific has been accomplished, but as long as students keep talking, you're on the right track.

9. Be willing to role model everything, but beware of sharing your personal experiences too often and in too much detail. Remember that this is *their* group, not yours. The role modeling you do should be for the purpose of facilitating student responses. Too much can *inhibit* response. You might not need to role model most of the activity sheets, especially if they are self-explanatory and if there are time constraints. (An example of an activity sheet that requires role modeling is "Giving Myself Permission.")

10. Be alert to moments when it is wise to protect students from each other and themselves. For example, if a group member begins with something like, "I've never said this to anybody—it's about something pretty bad that happened to me...," you may want to encourage him or her to pause before continuing ("Are you comfortable about sharing this with the group?"). Ask the group, "Are you ready to be trusted? Remember what we said about confidentiality."

11. In situations where members of the group verbally attack each other, another kind of protection may be needed, namely leader intervention. The group can also process what has happened by sharing their feelings about the conflict.

12. If a student reacts emotionally with momentary discomfort or tears, offer verbal support, a tissue (if handy), or a touch (a pat on the arm, perhaps, or a hug, *if* the student has indicated that touch is all right). Encourage group members to do likewise. Be aware that some students may not want to be touched at all.

13. If conflict arises among members of the group, use the group process to deal with it. This is an excellent time to talk honestly about feelings and to demonstrate conflict resolution. Invite the group to tell how they feel about the conflict.

14. Listen carefully to the student who is speaking, but also be sure to monitor nonverbal behavior in the entire group. Be alert to those who are not speaking. Are they showing discomfort (averted eyes, moving back, facial tics), frustration (agitation, head-shaking, mumbled negatives), or anxiety (uneasy eyes, unsteady hands, tense face)?

15. Be honest and sincere in your comments, commendations, and compliments. Watch for and act on opportunities to tell students that they have done well, especially in articulating complex feelings and situations ("You put words on a very complex feeling." "You explained that very well").

endings

Each session includes a suggestion for closure. If you complete the session and the closure and still have time left over, you might use it to begin the next writing activity, or to ask questions designed to encourage thinking about the next session or focus.

At the end of a group experience—whether a short series of sessions or an entire year of meetings—it is wise to purposefully wind down. The Follow-Up on page 20 can be used to conclude a series of meetings.

Most important in any final session, and possibly over the last few sessions, is the need for participants to talk about what they have experienced in the group. I have found that asking students to write a few paragraphs during a final session is helpful. Sometimes, when group attendance was voluntary, I have asked, "Why did you keep coming to the group?" At other times, I have simply invited students to talk about what they have gained in personal insights, what they have learned about adolescence in general, what areas of common ground they have discovered, and how they have changed over the period of time the group has met.

All groups, whatever their size and duration, need to prepare for the time when the group will no longer meet. Most students miss the group when it is done, and they feel a sense of loss. Especially if they have grown to depend on the group for support, they may feel anxious about facing the future without the group. If they have learned to know others well through the group, and if they have made friends, they may wonder if they will lose touch once the group disbands.

A few sessions prior to ending, mention casually that there are only a few meetings remaining. Continue to do that until the next-to-last session. At that time, you might mention what you have in mind for the final session, or ask the group for suggestions. You might plan a party, have food brought in, and/or take a group photo.

Be sure to leave time at the final session for them, and you, to say goodbye. If it is possible that they will not have much future contact with each other, provide a way for them to share addresses and wish each other well. Be aware that you will be role modeling, and offering strategies for, ending what has likely been a profound experience. For many people—adults and teenagers—that is a difficult process.

It is not always easy to "read" a group and to know whether it is moving in a positive direction. Individuals who readily and frequently give feedback cannot speak for everyone. Quiet members may be gaining insights that they simply aren't sharing. A session that seemed to generate an indifferent or poor response might, in fact, have made an impact, but it may not be apparent. Groups are complex, and members differ in their needs and what they respond to. Therefore, it is wise periodically to have group members fill out an evaluation, particularly at the end of the group experience.

On pages 21–23, you will find a Discussion Group Evaluation form to copy and use. (Start by making one copy for yourself, then fill in the names of the applicable sessions and make copies for your group.) Or you might choose to create your own form, depending on what you hope to learn and tailoring the questions to your group. Feedback provided on such evaluations can be invaluable when assessing past groups and planning for future groups.

permission for student participation

Dear Parent,

I have invited your son or daughter to participate in a discussion group at school. The purpose of the group is to provide adolescents with an opportunity to gain skills in articulating common social and emotional concerns. Such skills are important in all relationships, from friendship to marriage, college roommate relationships, relationships with co-workers, and parenting. The groups are also designed to promote self-awareness during a period when young people are establishing their identity and preparing to move into adulthood.

Adolescence is a time of stress in even the best of situations. Not only are there physical changes; there are new feelings and emotions to deal with as well. It is a time of increasing awareness of others' expectations. There are also new opportunities for involvement at school, and there are academic choices to be made. Relationships take on new dimensions.

Our discussion group will focus on social and emotional concerns. Even though we may discuss academics in terms of stress or procrastination, for example, the group will be far different from the often competitive academic world. Students will relax with each other and find out what they have in common. They will learn how to communicate support to each other. They will become acquainted with classmates in their group—for the first time, perhaps, or simply better than before.

If your child participates, you may soon notice positive growth both at school and at home. There may be positive changes in communication. Talking about stress, developing strategies for problem-solving, gaining a clearer sense of self, feeling the support of trusted peers—all of these experiences in the group should contribute to enhanced self-esteem and life satisfaction as your son or daughter navigates adolescence.

The group will begin very soon. If you give your permission for your child to be involved, and if your child decides to participate, please sign below and return the form to me as soon as possible. If you have any questions, please call me at _____.

_____ has my permission to participate in the discussion group.
    (Name of child)

_____
    (Parent signature)

_____
    (Date)

group guidelines

The purpose of this group is to "just talk"—to share our thoughts, feelings, and concerns with each other in an atmosphere of mutual trust, caring, and understanding. To make this group successful and meaningful, we agree to the following terms and guidelines.

1. Anything that is said in the group stays in the group. We agree to keep things absolutely confidential. This means we don't share information outside of the group. We agree to do our part, individually and together, to make this group a safe place to talk.

2. We respect what other group members say. We agree not to use put-downs of any kind, verbal or nonverbal. Body language, facial expressions, and sighs can all be put-downs, and we agree to control our own behavior so that everyone feels valued and accepted.

3. We respect everyone's need to be heard. We agree that no one will dominate the group. We understand that just because someone is quiet or shy doesn't mean he or she has nothing to say. We also know that active listening and keen observation are valuable skills.

4. We listen to each other. When someone is speaking, we look at him or her and pay attention. We use supportive and encouraging body language and facial expressions.

5. We realize that feelings are not "bad" or "good." They just *are*. Therefore, we don't say things like "You shouldn't feel that way."

6. We are willing to take risks, to explore new ideas, and to explain our feelings as well as we can. However, we agree that someone who doesn't *want* to talk doesn't *have* to talk. We don't force people to share when they don't feel comfortable sharing.

7. We are willing to let others know us. We agree that talking and listening are ways for people to get to know each other.

8. We realize that sometimes people feel misunderstood, or they feel that someone has hurt them accidentally or on purpose. We agree that the best way to handle those times is by talking and listening. If someone feels hurt or misunderstood, we want him or her to express those feelings and explore where they come from. We encourage assertiveness.

9. We agree to be honest and to do our best to speak from the heart.

10. We don't talk about group members who aren't present. We *especially* don't criticize group members who aren't here to defend themselves.

11. When we do need to talk about other people—such as teachers and peers—we don't refer to them by name unless it is absolutely necessary. For example, we may want to ask the group to help us solve a problem we are having with a particular person.

12. We agree to attend group meetings regularly. We don't want to miss information that might be referred to later. Most of all, we know that we are important to the group. If for some reason we can't attend a meeting, we will try to let the leader know ahead of time.

warm-up

Name: _____

Complete these sentences:

1. I've heard that this group _____
   _____
   _____
   _____

2. I hope the group will _____
   _____
   _____
   _____

3. Probably the most interesting thing about
   me is_____
   _____
   _____
   _____

4. Something I have that is very special to
   me is_____
   _____
   _____
   _____

5. I'm good at_____
   _____
   _____
   _____

6. I've never been able to _____
   _____
   _____
   _____

7. A really dramatic moment in my life was
   when _____
   _____
   _____
   _____

8. Probably the biggest accomplishment of
   my life so far is _____
   _____
   _____
   _____

9. I like people who_____
   _____
   _____
   _____

10. I'm probably most myself when I _____
    _____
    _____
    _____

11. You probably wouldn't believe that I
    _____
    _____
    _____
    _____

12. The time of day I'm most alert is _____
    _____
    _____
    _____

13. I'm looking forward to_____
    _____
    _____
    _____

14. I can imagine myself someday_____
    _____
    _____
    _____

follow-up

Name: _____

Complete these sentences with words, phrases, paragraphs—anything goes!

1. Who am I? At this point in my life, I am
   _____
   _____
   _____
   _____

2. As I leave this group, I feel good that
   _____
   _____
   _____
   _____

3. I regret that I didn't _____
   _____

4. I hope that I _____
   _____

5. Someone in the group I'm glad I know
   better is _____
   _____

6. An important topic for me was_____
   _____

7. Something important that I learned was
   _____
   _____
   _____

8. A very interesting experience in the group
   was_____
   _____
   _____
   _____

9. I feel more aware of _____
   _____
   _____
   _____

10. I discovered that I _____
    _____
    _____

11. I learned that others _____
    _____
    _____

12. I also learned that _____
    _____
    _____

13. I was surprised that_____
    _____
    _____

14. I learned to appreciate _____
    _____
    _____

15. During this experience, I probably
    changed in_____
    _____
    _____
    _____

16. During this whole year, I've probably
    changed in_____
    _____
    _____
    _____

17. I will probably always remember _____
    _____
    _____
    _____

18. I am glad that I _____
    _____

discussion group evaluation

What did you think of the group experience? Your feedback is important! Your honest—and anonymous—responses and opinions will help future groups. Please complete and return this evaluation form. Thank you for your time.

PART ONE

Circle the number that best describes your feelings about each session.

1 = This session was very valuable and enjoyable to me.

2 = This session was worthwhile and fairly enjoyable to me.

3 = This session was "average"—"just okay."

4 = This session was not really valuable to me, and I didn't enjoy it much.

5 = This session was not valuable or enjoyable at all. I suggest that you don't include it in future groups.

6 = This session was not part of my group/I didn't participate in this session.

FOCUS: THE SELF

1 2 3 4 5 6 _____

1 2 3 4 5 6 _____

1 2 3 4 5 6 _____

1 2 3 4 5 6 _____

1 2 3 4 5 6 _____

1 2 3 4 5 6 _____

FOCUS: THE SELF AND OTHERS

1 2 3 4 5 6 _____

1 2 3 4 5 6 _____

1 2 3 4 5 6 _____

1 2 3 4 5 6 _____

1 2 3 4 5 6 _____

1 2 3 4 5 6 _____

FOCUS: STRESS

1 2 3 4 5 6 _____

1 2 3 4 5 6 _____

1 2 3 4 5 6 _____

1 2 3 4 5 6 _____

1 2 3 4 5 6 _____

1 2 3 4 5 6 _____

PART TWO

Look back at the list of discussion topics and circle the ones that were the most meaningful for you personally.

PART THREE

Circle the number that best describes how you would rate each of the following.

1 = excellent

2 = good

3 = average

4 = fair

5 = poor

1 2 3 4 5   The group experience as a whole.

1 2 3 4 5   The ability of the leader to guide the group.

1 2 3 4 5   The warmth and concern of the group leader.

1 2 3 4 5   The leader's respect for every member of the group.

1 2 3 4 5   The value of the group for people like me.

1 2 3 4 5   The value of the group for me personally.

1 2 3 4 5   The general level of comfort and emotional/personal safety in the group for sharing feelings.

1 2 3 4 5   The level of comfort and safety I felt in the group personally.

1 2 3 4 5   The respect I felt for the other members of my group.

1 2 3 4 5   The respect that the other members of my group showed toward me.

PART FOUR

*For each of these statements, circle your response ("would" or "wouldn't," "do" or "don't")
and give a reason.*

1. I would or wouldn't recommend this group to a friend because _____
   _____
   _____
   _____
   _____

2. If I had it to do over, I would or wouldn't participate in this group because _____
   _____
   _____
   _____
   _____

3. I would or wouldn't participate in another discussion group because _____
   _____
   _____
   _____
   _____

4. In general, I do or don't think discussion groups are very helpful because _____
   _____
   _____
   _____
   _____

PART FIVE

Additional comments:

_____
_____
_____
_____
_____
_____
_____

focus

the self

focus: the self

"I don't know who I am."

Spoken aloud or left unsaid, this is a common thought among people of all ages, especially adolescents. Developing a personal identity is an important task of adolescence.

Teenagers learn "who they are" through hearing what others say about them, identifying what they feel and value, and thinking about themselves in relationship with others. However, they often get mixed messages—from parents, peers, teachers, and others. Sometimes they receive mostly negative messages and let these "define" them. Adults who model for them how to relate to others may not be good models, and the adolescents in turn may behave in ways that prevent their getting positive messages about themselves. Depending on who their friends are, their gender, and their family experiences, teens may have little opportunity to talk about their doubts, fears, and hopes. They also might be unable to articulate such thoughts and feelings, not having had much practice with either family or peers.

Confusion and doubt about the self can lead to tension, inappropriate behavior, and acting out. Frustration about the self can cause trouble in relationships. Not knowing the self can interfere with finding career direction.

Group discussions give teens an opportunity to gain skill in articulating thoughts and feelings. As you work with your group, remind them of how important this skill can be, both for their lives today and for the future. Talking about what is "inside" is good practice for quality friendships, for getting along with co-workers, for marriage, and for being parents. Explain that sharing their thoughts and feelings in a group can also help them to discover what they have in common and to understand that they are not as different or as "weird" as they might believe. Finding out what they think and feel through talking moves them along in the process of self-discovery. Group discussions can help them answer a vital question, "Who am I?"

general objectives

- Students make progress in defining themselves as individuals, separate from family and friends.

- They learn to articulate thoughts and feelings.

- They discover what they think and feel by sharing thoughts and feelings with the group and receiving and evaluating feedback from the group.

- Feedback from the group helps them to clarify and evaluate their opinions, beliefs, and values.

- They apply to their own self-assessment what others share.

focus: the self
personal strengths and limitations

- Through articulating personal strengths, students affirm their capabilities and enhance their self-esteem.

- By sharing their personal limitations with peers and getting feedback, students learn that others have similar weaknesses and that having limitations is not "shameful."

- Students increase their self-awareness and ability to assess themselves realistically.

- They learn to value their unique strengths and to see that there are many kinds of valuable personal characteristics.

- They learn that they do not have to apologize for their strengths or their limitations.

1. Have the students list on paper their personal strengths. Tell them to think of the things they can "count on" or "have confidence in" or "trust" about themselves, both as they interact with others and when they are alone. You might also ask, "What do you think other people value in you?" Share your own list and/or offer suggestions from this list.

organized	a good listener
responsible	kind
compassionate	energetic
personable	even-tempered
patient	an eager learner
athletic	a good dancer
helpful	not moody
intelligent	good sense of humor
wit	verbal or mathematical skills
mechanical gifts	musical or other artistic talent
good with elderly people and/or young children	

Tell the students that affirming their capabilities is good practice for the future, when they will need to speak or write about themselves with confidence during job interviews, on scholarship and award application forms, and on essays in the college application process.

2. Encourage the students to share their lists.

Adolescents usually are willing to share their lists, even when the group is just beginning and before it has developed a good level of trust and comfort. Contributions help to "build a group." However, be sure to remind group members that they always have the right to "pass" on any part of this and future sessions they feel uncomfortable sharing.

3. Have the students list on paper their personal limitations. Tell them to think of the characteristics, habits, and "flaws" that get in the way of things they want to do; that cause problems in their relationships; that keep them from being their best. Share your own list and/or offer suggestions from this list.

a procrastinator	bad-tempered
a gossip	disorganized
impatient	irresponsible
messy	mean
a poor listener	critical
naive	easily depressed

4. Encourage the students to share their lists.

5. If the students are able to list more limitations than strengths, don't be surprised. Time permitting, discuss why this might happen.

6. For closure, ask the students which strengths and limitations seem to be common in the group. Ask, "How did it feel to talk about your strengths and limitations with the other group members?"

focus: the self
three selves

objectives

- Students experience an honest appraisal of themselves in the presence of supportive peers.

- Students thoughtfully compare their "real," their "disliked," and their "ideal" selves and assess how different or similar these three selves are.

- They receive helpful feedback from the group and learn how others see them.

suggestions

1. Have the students complete the "My Three Selves" activity sheet (page 32). Tell them that they may use adjectives, descriptive phrases, or sentences to describe themselves.

2. Encourage them to share their lists.

3. Ask the students to study their lists. Ask questions like the following.

   - Are your lists for "The Way I Really Am" and "The Self I'd Like to Be" fairly similar or very different?

   - Can you live with the parts of the self you don't like? Does someone you don't appreciate have these traits? Are these traits really so terrible?

   - Are the traits listed under "The Self I'd Like to Be" really possible for you? Maybe some are and some aren't. For those that are possible, what can you do to get closer to being that way?

   - Can you accept your "real" self?

   - What would you like to change about yourself?

4. For closure, ask the group to comment on what was valuable about this session. If appropriate, commend the group for their honesty and supportive comments.

my three selves

Name: _____

List adjectives or phrases under each heading.

THE WAY I REALLY AM

1. _____
2. _____
3. _____
4. _____
5. _____

THE SELF I DON'T LIKE

1. _____
2. _____
3. _____
4. _____
5. _____

THE SELF I'D LIKE TO BE

1. _____
2. _____
3. _____
4. _____
5. _____

The two lists which are most alike for me are _____

_____

If I could "try on" a new image, I think I would like to _____

_____

_____

focus: the self
behind the facade

Adolescents often speak of "hypocrites" and "phoneys." They like to use the word "real"—as in "be real," "not being real." They are quick to judge others as insincere. They are disgusted by "fake smiles" and gossip about status-seeking behavior. They sneer at teachers and administrators who claim to be interested in individual students but can't remember their names. They might even speak of "putting on a front"—for the sake of impressing teachers or getting into the right social circle. They probably have strong words for such behavior. Yet, in spite of their judging, they probably wear a facade of some kind themselves, as do we all.

Most adolescents are aware that facial expression and behavior communicate a great deal. They might hide their own sadness and important needs behind smiles and congeniality "because no one wants to be around sad people." With a blank, cold, or negative facade, they send strong messages: "leave me alone" or "don't mess with me." A no-worry demeanor might studiously hide anxiety.

Students know about "fronts." They know that facades are part of interacting with their world. Perhaps they are more "real" at home than at school or at work—or perhaps not.

objectives

- Students look honestly at the facade(s) they wear in various social situations.

- They discover similarities within the group, particularly in regard to kinds and functions of social faces.

- They learn to articulate feelings and important personal thoughts.

- They learn that sharing doubts and other feelings enhances trust in the group.

suggestions

1. Begin with general questions such as the following.

   ▶ What is a "facade"? (If students have never heard the word, explain that it means a "front," like a storefront. It may be deceptive, and it may put a new "face" on whatever is behind it.)

   ▶ How can the word "facade" relate to people?

> Do most, or all, people put on a "social face" when they are not at home? Is it a necessity?

> In your opinion, how different are most people's facades from their "real" selves?

> Why do you think someone might wear a facade? What social purpose does a facade serve?

> Do we sometimes hide our "real" selves behind a facade? What would happen if we didn't do that?

2. Move the discussion from the general to the specific. You might begin by saying something like this: "If it's normal to wear a facade, let's think about what kind of social face we might be wearing now, in this group."

At this point you might tell the group what kind of "face" you are wearing at the moment. Perhaps it is the kind of face—and behavior—you usually have on in your professional setting. You may want it to show that you are interested, warm, and compassionate. You probably want to seem alert and energetic.

After describing your "face," ask questions like the following.

> What is *your* "social facade"? Do you have more than one?

> What purpose does it serve?

> Does it ever cause problems for you or the people around you?

> What would your peers or teachers discover about you if you didn't wear a social face?

3. Direct the discussion to consideration of places where students feel comfortable and do not need to wear facades. Ask questions like the following.

> Where can you take off your facade?

> What are you like when it is off? Is there more or less variety in your facial expression and behavior when it is off?

> How many people here in school (or whatever the setting) know what you are like without your facade?

> Are the people who know the "real" you more, or less, respectful of you than those who don't?

4. Invite the group to consider how and when facades begin to develop. Ask questions like the following.

> Do little children have facades?

> How do we respond to small children's spontaneous, natural, innocent, personal, too-direct comments? Do we like them?

> When do children start to become more "socially aware" and less spontaneous?

> What causes that to happen?

> ❯ How do you respond to one of your peers who seems more childlike than the rest of you? Is it "shameful" to be childlike at your age?

> ❯ Do you think that adults have "thicker" facades than people your age? What are you basing your comments on?

> ❯ What is good about the "social face"?

> ❯ What is not so good about it?

> ❯ Is there a danger that a facade could keep others from knowing when someone needs support and help?

5. For closure, ask for a volunteer to share one or two thoughts about the session—either the content of the session or the process of discussing it. The students might consider whether the group seemed relaxed and open, or tense and tight-lipped, about the topic. Did most people share willingly? Was it an uncomfortable topic? Is it something they think about often? How did it feel to talk about how we present ourselves socially?

focus: the self
does the stereotype fit?

- Students learn about the problems, limitations, and dangers of thinking in stereotypes.
- They learn about themselves by considering how they do and do not fit stereotypes that are applied to them.

1. Especially if your group is relatively young, find out if they understand what a "stereotype" is. Ask for volunteers to define the term and give examples.

   If necessary, define it for them. You might say something like this: "A stereotype is an idea that many people share about a particular group of people. It is a way of describing and defining the people in that group without really knowing anything about them as individuals. For example, you may have heard that all rich people are snobs, or all poor people are lazy. These are stereotypes. They affect the way we think about rich people and poor people. They affect the way we treat them. Stereotypes also affect the way we think about ourselves, when we are aware that others are stereotyping us."

2. Ask the students to think about how they might be stereotyped at school. Provide a few examples to get them started: "jock," "nerd," "dumb blonde," "underachiever," "brain," "teacher's pet." To model, share an example of a stereotype that has been used to describe you at some point in your life.

3. Encourage the students to share their words or phrases. You may hear some or all of the following (or whatever terms are currently in vogue).

rebel	from the wrong side of town
dumb farmer	doctor's kid
skateboarder	motorhead
only child	from a single-parent home
lazy	snob
stereotypes related to ethnic background or religious affiliation	into drugs/alcohol

36

4. For each student who chooses to share how he or she might be stereotyped, ask the group, "Does the stereotype fit _____ (name of student)?" Then ask the student, "What do you think? Do you fit the stereotype? Why or why not?"

5. After that round of sharing, continue by asking the students one or more of the following questions. You might want to move around the group in order, so that each student has a chance to be heard.

   ▶ What do you wish people in general understood about you?

   ▶ What do you wish your classmates understood about you?

   ▶ What do you wish your teachers understood about you?

   ▶ What do you wish your parents understood about you?

   If time permits and the group seems interested, invite discussion about "feeling misunderstood."

6. For closure, either summarize the session yourself or ask the students to tell what they might have learned or felt during the discussion. Ask if anything they heard surprised them or caused them to examine their own thinking—and maybe even change their thinking in some way.

focus: the self
going to extremes

- Students learn that most people—even those who seem the most secure—are somewhat distressed about being "too" something.

- They learn to articulate their own concerns about being "too" something.

- They hear how others perceive their "too" characteristics and discover that these might even be considered advantages rather than liabilities.

suggestions

1. Introduce the topic by sharing with the students a "too" characteristic of your own. Perhaps you believe that you are "too" stressed, disorganized, impatient, or restless.

2. Invite the students to share their "toos"—something they *are* "too much" or "too little," or *do* "too much" or "too little." Or have the students list their "toos" on paper and then share them. Responses might include the following.

shy	talkative
loud	clumsy
lazy	easily distracted
lonely	people-pleasing
"driven"	nervous
rebellious	depressed

3. Ask the students how these characteristics might, in fact, have some advantages. Give them several seconds to ponder that possibility.

   For example, shyness might be perceived as "mysterious," a positive and intriguing trait that some people find attractive. Shy people might be more comfortable alone than extroverts. They might be able to work more quietly and effectively on a long-term project. They probably think before acting. They may be better at finding strength from within, instead of relying on others to help them through hard times. Ask how many students consider themselves to be "shy" in social situations. This may begin a good discussion.

4. If the students listed their "toos" on paper, and if they feel comfortable sharing what they wrote, have them exchange lists with the person sitting next to them. Have each student write or comment on the possible advantages of the other person's "toos."

5. For closure, ask for summary statements about "too" characteristics and other "bothersome traits." Ask, "What did you learn from each other today? What are some things you have in common? How did it feel to discuss being 'too . . .'?"

focus: the self
perfectionism

Perfectionism can be seen as a positive trait. It drives people to do a good job and to set high standards, and it may lead to headlines and praise. However, the list of positives probably ends there. A list of negatives is much longer.

Perfectionism does not encourage risk-taking, whether academic, personal, or social. It is hard for perfectionists to enjoy the present, the "process," or a job well done because of a preoccupation with "product" and "next time." They are self-critical, competitive, and critical of others, and their perfectionism often interferes with relationships.

Perfectionists are often preoccupied with others' expectations—or the expectations within themselves. They often set impossible and unrealistic goals, and they tend to feel their worth in what they do, rather than in just "being." Many are prone to depression.

We probably want our surgeon, our dentist, our banker, and our mechanic to be perfectionists in their work, but we probably don't want to have a perfectionist for a roommate, to be married to one, or to be taught by one.

Many gifted students are perfectionistic and highly self-critical. They need to discuss perfectionism, as they are sometimes debilitated by it both in the academic world and in their personal lives. Sometimes gifted individuals do not achieve in school because they feel they cannot perform at a certain level of perfection or because they refuse to be involved in a situation that is not "ideal." If they are high achievers, perfectionism can interfere with their ability to enjoy life, as well as cause high stress. Acceptance and love in relationships might be seen as conditional.

Perfectionism can come in many forms. It can demand a spotless house, closet, or room; an unblemished piece of writing; an unflawed relationship; an ideal day; a perfect performance; a test with no errors; a perfect friend; no attempt until success can be assured; a perfect product. It causes great tension.

The perfectionist cycle can be broken—first by recognizing the tendencies, and then by encouraging new experiences, participation in "ungraded" activities, self-talk about not connecting worth to performance, reducing compulsive planning, conscious acceptance of less-than-perfect performances and products, eliminating "should" from one's personal vocabulary, and setting realistic standards.

recommended resource

Adderholdt-Elliott, Miriam, *Perfectionism: What's Bad about Being Too Good?* (Minneapolis: Free Spirit Publishing, 1987). Explains the differences between healthy ambition and unhealthy perfectionism and gives strategies for getting out of the perfectionist trap. For ages 13 and up.

objectives

- Students learn that perfectionism can be both a blessing and a curse.
- They practice articulating feelings and behaviors—in this case, concerning perfectionism.
- They explore alternatives to perfectionism.
- They consider the sources of their own perfectionism.
- They brainstorm strategies for combating perfectionism.

suggestions

1. Introduce the topic of perfectionism and invite group members to share ways in which they might be perfectionists. Ask, "What is something you always feel you have to do perfectly?"

2. Ask, "What is *good* about perfectionism?" Students may respond that it can result in good grades, high performance, respect and adulation from others, praise from parents and teachers, and the drive to "do better" and "be better."

3. Ask, "What is *bad* about perfectionism?" If students don't contribute the following ideas, offer some to the discussion.

   Perfectionists sometimes or often...

   . . . set unreasonable, impossible goals for themselves

   . . . can't be satisfied with even a great result and may, in fact, be chronically dissatisfied

   . . . have difficulty enjoying the present moment because they are preoccupied with overcoming the next "hurdle"

   . . . are not risk-takers (academically and/or socially) because they fear "failing," "not being the best," and "not doing it well enough"

   . . . have an "all-or-nothing" view: "If I can't do it perfectly, there's no point in doing it at all"

   . . . are highly self-critical and preoccupied with their own and others' expectations

   . . . are critical of others

   . . . are highly competitive and are constantly comparing themselves to others

   . . . experience stress and anxiety

   . . . are afraid of making mistakes

. . . are afraid of revealing their weaknesses or imperfections

. . . procrastinate because of their need to do something "perfectly"

. . . might spend a lot of time and energy doing something over (and over and over) until it's "perfect"

. . . are prone to depression

. . . have difficulty in relationships because they expect too much of themselves and others

. . . feel that their self-worth depends on "performance," and therefore are very sensitive to criticism and are afraid to just "be"

. . . cannot accept that love can be unconditional

. . . are compulsive planners

. . . have difficulty seeing situations, performances, and projects in terms other than "good" or "bad"

. . . are dissatisfied with situations and relationships that are not "ideal"

4. Tell students to consider their answers to the question from suggestion #1 ("What is something you always feel you have to do perfectly?"). Ask, "What do you think would happen if you *didn't* do that particular thing perfectly? What's the *worst* thing that could happen?" If they voice fears about "what _____ would think," someone who might be "disappointed," or someone who might notice and comment on their "imperfect" performance, encourage them to explore their fears by "putting words on them."

   If your group consists of gifted students who are also underachievers, recognize that they probably wrestle with perfectionism, too, and encourage them to participate. While feelings of inadequacy may motivate high achievers, they can cause underachievers to give up and withdraw from the competition inherent in the academic world. Underachievers may fear making mistakes as much as achievers do.

5. Ask, "If you're a perfectionist, where do you think your perfectionism comes from? Does the 'push' to be perfect come from within you, or from others? If from others, what do they say?" (It might have been simply *assumed*. Or their fear of error may actually *invite* criticism.) Introduce the following ideas if they don't come up in the discussion. Ask the students if these statements fit their situations.

   ▶ People (parents, teachers, other adults, friends) expect me to be perfect.

   ▶ I'm supposed to be the "perfect child" in my family. (NOTE: You may want to explore this issue further. For example, you might ask, "Have you always played that role? Are other people in your family allowed to make mistakes? Who told you to be the perfect child?")

   ▶ I worry about letting other people down.

> If I'm not perfect, I get criticized.

> Everything around me is in chaos. Being perfect is the only way to get things under control.

> I have to be perfect for people to like me and accept me.

6. Invite the students to brainstorm strategies for combating perfectionism. Some suggestions follow.

> Be average for a day. Give yourself permission to be messy, late, incomplete...imperfect. Then celebrate your "success."

> Get involved in activities that are not graded or judged—that focus on process, not product. (NOTE: You may want to take this opportunity to discuss a "process" approach to life. For example, people and skills are forever "being made." It's also possible to enjoy simply being *involved* in something, with no "end" in mind.)

> Take a risk. Sign up for a course with a reputation for being a challenge. Smile and start a conversation with someone you don't know. Do an assignment or study for a test without "overdoing" it. Alter your morning routine. Start a day without a plan.

> Give yourself permission to make at least three mistakes a day. Smile at them.

> Stop using the word "should" in your self-talk. Remove "I have to" from your conversation.

> Share a "weakness" or "limitation" with a friend. Recognize that he or she doesn't think any less of you as a result.

> Acknowledge that your expectations of yourself might be too high, even unrealistic.

> Find out more about perfectionism. Ask about it; read about it.

> Trace the roots of your own perfectionism. Try to understand when and where it all started. With comments heard at home or school? With wanting to win approval or avoid disapproval?

> Savor your past accomplishments.

> Ask your friends to help you "cure" your perfectionism. Perhaps they can give you a sign or a word when they notice you are being perfectionistic.

> Tell yourself repeatedly that it's okay to be less than perfect—in fact, it's unavoidable, because nobody's perfect.

> Join the human race. It's less lonely when we accept our own and others' imperfections and feel part of *life*. We are all in it together.

> Lighten up!

7. For closure, ask, "What would happen if you stopped trying to be perfect in your area of perfectionism?" Or have them choose an "anti-perfectionism" task from the list of strategies brainstormed in suggestion #6. Ask them how they felt during the discussion.

focus: the self
intensity, compulsivity, and moderation

background

It's fun for students to compare notes on their interests and passions. Especially for students who may have had no one to share an interest with, this experience can be affirming and celebratory. They learn that they're not alone, and that their intensity isn't "weird."

If your group consists of gifted students, it helps to be aware that intensity and giftedness often go hand-in-hand. Whether it's dinosaurs, the solar system, science fiction, Dungeons & Dragons, baseball cards, Presidents, science, writing, drawing, ballet, ham radio, LEGO blocks, gymnastics, basketball, computers, video games, or another area of interest, gifted students sometimes take it to the limit. They read everything they can find about it, think and talk about it constantly, fill their rooms with it, and try the patience of their parents and teachers—until they move on to something else and the cycle starts all over again.

For students of all ability levels, some passions may last a lifetime, leading to a meaningful career and great accomplishments. Compulsivity, however, is another matter. Students (and adults, of course) sometimes become so involved in an interest or activity that it takes over their lives. People can become compulsive workers, eaters, "neatniks," readers, runners, and shoppers. They can become compulsive about exercise, cleanliness, and socializing. An open and honest discussion can sometimes help students to take stock of such behaviors and move toward moderation in areas where compulsivity is a problem.

objectives

- Students learn that many others have experienced periods in their lives when they were passionate about a particular interest or activity.
- They learn the difference between intensity and compulsivity.
- They consider the value of moderation and brainstorm ways to gain control over a compulsion.

suggestions

1. Introduce the topic and ask group members if they can recall a "passion" from the past—a topic or activity they were intensely interested in and spent a lot of time pursuing. Ask questions like the following of those with such experiences.

   ▸ Who did you share this passion with?

   ▸ How did your parents feel about your passion?

   ▸ Was your passion connected to school in any way?

   ▸ Did you feel that you learned or experienced everything you could about your passion?

   ▸ When did your passion diminish? Did you eventually "burn out" on it or simply move on to something else?

   ▸ If this is typical for you, how long does one of your passions usually last?

   You might tell the group that such intensity often has contributed to important discoveries in science, to excellence and high achievement, and to the broad knowledge that is the foundation for research and social progress. These are some of the positives of being passionately interested in something.

2. Encourage the students to talk about their current passions and related experiences.

3. Turn the discussion to the topic of compulsivity. Remind the group of the need for confidentiality; some students may share sensitive information, and they should know that it will be safe to do so. Ask questions like the following.

   ▸ Has anything ever prevented you from following an interest or passion? What happened? How did you deal with it? How did you feel about it?

   ▸ Have you ever become so deeply involved in an interest or activity that it got in the way of your relationships? That it affected your health? Your school performance? Your home life?

   ▸ How did you find out that your passion was causing problems? Did somebody tell you, or did you realize it on your own?

   ▸ Was there anyone who helped you to gain perspective on the situation? What did that person say or do?

4. Invite the students to brainstorm ways to gain control over a compulsion. Following are some suggestions.

   ▸ Limit the time you spend each day on your interest. Set an alarm; when it goes off, go on to something else.

   ▸ Explore other areas of interest so that no single area becomes all-important.

   ▸ Don't forget to stay connected to people.

> ❯ Talk to your parents. Ask them if they think you are spending too much time on your interest.

> ❯ If you feel that your passion is taking over your life, or if you are concerned about the level of your involvement, talk to an adult that you trust.

5. For closure, invite the group to summarize the session. Ask what their thoughts are about intense interests in general—or about theirs in particular—now that these "passions" have been discussed. Ask what they discovered they have in common.

focus: the self
learning styles

Some people prefer to learn by listening, some by seeing, some by doing. Some like information to be presented sequentially and in a structured environment, while others seem to thrive in a kinetic, richly textured, unpredictable environment, where information is coming at them from many directions and sources simultaneously. Some students need to like the teacher in order to do well; for others, this is irrelevant to their learning. Some students are easily distracted; others focus easily. Some sit in the front; others head for the back. Some like group work while others prefer to work alone.

When teaching style and learning style are at odds, problems may result. However, both the teacher and the student may be unaware that some of the problems may be related to their differing styles. Similarly, when teaching and learning styles are a match, good progress is likely. Unfortunately, most teachers teach largely in their own preferred style. They need to be encouraged to teach in their unpreferred modes as well in order to accommodate learning styles that differ from theirs.

It is a common assumption that most disciplinary referrals are kinesthetic learners, referred by non-kinesthetic teachers, yet few teachers examine whether an adjustment in teaching method would improve the situation. Long-term projects and written work are often difficult for such students. Yet these same troublesome kinesthetic learners might nevertheless enjoy school, have good health, and do well in life as adults.

This session can help students understand why they appreciate some teachers more than others, and why they might be having trouble in some classes. Through becoming informed, they might become more assertive in asking teachers to modify teaching methods in specific ways in order to help students like them.

You might want to keep a record of the various learning styles that become apparent through the continuum exercise used in this session or through the use of an assessment such as the Gregorc instrument; see Recommended Resources. Such information can be valuable in advocating changes in the classroom for underachieving students.

recommended resources

Gregorc, Anthony F., *The Gregorc Style Delineator*, a learning style self-assessment, and *An Adult's Guide to Style*. Available from Gregorc Associates, Inc., P.O. Box 351, Columbia, CT 06237; (203) 228-0093. Dr. Anthony F. Gregorc is a leader in identifying and clarifying learning styles.

Butler, Kathleen A., *It's All in Your Mind: A Student Guide to Learning Style* and *A Teacher's Guide for It's All in Your Mind*. Available from The Learner's Dimension, P.O. Box 6, Columbia, CT 06237; (203) 228-3786. The student guide explains four main learning style types, with questionnaires to help readers discover their own learning (and teaching) style preferences. For ages 13 and up. The teacher's guide helps teachers plan lessons with a focus on style. Both books are based on original research by Dr. Anthony F. Gregorc.

objectives

- Students learn about various teaching and learning styles.
- They become more aware of their own preferred learning styles.
- They develop an understanding of why they may experience difficulties in certain learning situations and where they may want to consider trying to accommodate a style different from their own.

suggestions

1. Introduce the topic with some ideas from the background information. Point out that differing teacher and student styles sometimes cause problems in learning. Explain that learning style can also affect what courses students choose, what teachers are sought after, and what kinds of assignments are easiest to accomplish.

2. Have the students line up along one wall of the room (or form an angle along two sides). Tell the students that they have just formed a "continuum." Designate one end of the continuum as "to a great extent/a lot" and the other end as "not at all." Explain that you are going to read a series of statements about learning style. As you read each statement, the students should physically move to the point on the continuum that best represents where they feel they belong.

3. Read aloud each statement from "Learning Styles: A Continuum Activity" on page 50. After each statement, and after students have found their places on the continuum, select two or three students to explain why they placed themselves where they did. If time is short, do this only for selected statements. (NOTE: This is the kind of activity that needs to move along quickly, and it is best not to spend too long considering individual statements.)

4. For closure, ask the group if they can make a summary statement about themselves as a group. If they need help, ask questions like the following.

    ▶ Does this group have a collective "style"? If so, what is it?

    ▶ As a group, do you tend to prefer structured or unstructured learning situations?

▶ Would you rather learn in a variety of ways or primarily one way?

▶ As a group, are you easily distracted?

▶ Do you prefer working in groups or working alone?

▶ Do you learn best by doing, seeing, or listening?

It might be interesting to ask how your management of the group suits their individual or group styles. Is there anything you as leader should try to do differently? Could do differently? Finally, you might encourage the students to strengthen their "unpreferred modes." The more flexible they are, the easier it will be for them to learn and feel comfortable in all types of learning situations.

learning styles

1. I prefer to learn by doing—building, measuring, drawing, mixing, or fixing—instead of by listening or viewing.

2. I prefer to learn by listening—teacher presentations, speakers, audio tapes.

3. I prefer to learn by viewing or seeing—reading, overheads, films, chalkboard information.

4. I need to write something down to remember it.

5. I like to know what to expect in a class.

6. I like to know the purpose of what I am doing in a class.

7. I prefer classes that are highly structured.

8. I like classrooms that have many interesting and colorful things on the walls and elsewhere around the room.

9. I like to work in groups.

10. I like to debate issues.

11. I can tolerate a lot of information coming at me from many directions at once.

12. I like to have my teachers know me well.

13. I like to have teachers call on me and give me attention in class.

14. I learn best when I like the teacher, and I don't do as well when I don't like the teacher.

15. I easily accept authority in others.

16. I am easily distracted.

17. I like to sit in the front of a class.

18. I feel anxious and agitated when a class is disorderly.

19. I like to show what I know in class.

20. I prefer to work alone.

21. I can work and concentrate in the midst of a lot of noise or activity.

22. I try to do well in school because I don't like criticism.

23. I like to argue just for the sake of argument.

24. Most of my teachers like me.

focus: the self
who and what defines us?

Adolescents receive many messages from their environment. In fact, they have been receiving messages all through their lives—comments from fathers, mothers, siblings, friends, teachers, coaches, people who like them, people who don't like them, doctors, counselors, the media, and any number of other sources. They also receive messages from their test scores and grades.

Not all of these messages are positive and encouraging. Loving, nurturing, patient, secure parents send messages—but so do angry, preoccupied, frustrated, alienated, competitive, perfectionistic parents. Comments from people children care about—from family members as well as from peers— may be received as personal "definitions." Negatives are often internalized more readily and permanently than positives.

Gifted students are often "defined" as high-achieving, make-everyone-proud performers, with no concerns except getting good grades. Underachievers may be "defined" as lazy students who "don't care about school or the future." Students at risk may be "defined" as troublemakers; those with low ability may be "defined" as dull or slow.

This discussion provides an opportunity for all students to think about who or what has "defined" them. Whether gifted, average, or below average, achiever or underachiever, rebel or conformist, all students can benefit by looking at the sources of their personal definitions. Other group members and a leader who listens without judgment or criticism can send positive, supportive messages that might contribute to a new definition.

objectives

- Students learn that messages from significant people in their lives have the potential of defining them, for better or for worse.
- Within the supportive group environment, students examine those messages that have had an impact on their self-definition and self-esteem.

suggestions

1. Introduce the session with ideas from the background information. Ask the students to think about individuals in their lives who have made either positive or negative comments that have had an impact on them—their mothers, fathers, sisters, brothers, other relatives, teachers, coaches, friends, enemies, competitors, and so on. Be patient and unrushed as they ponder this request.

2. Have the students write down the most powerfully *positive* message anyone has ever given them—in words either written or spoken. They might also write down the most powerfully *negative* message anyone has ever given them—in words written or spoken.

3. Encourage the students to share what they have written. Respect the wishes of those who may prefer not to share the negative messages. Simply listen and acknowledge their messages with a nod and a smile (or a wince). Or you might contribute brief comments such as "Yes, that's positive!" or "That must have hurt!"

4. When this discussion slows down, ask the students to think about the negative messages. Ask, "Have those messages had an effect on you? If so, how could you hear them less powerfully now? If not, how have you not let them define you?"

5. Turn the group's attention to other sources of definition. Ask, "What other things or people in your environment tell you about yourselves?" Remind them that teachers are fallible, grading systems are flawed, siblings and peers may have "hidden agendas," some students do not "test well," and even "intelligence tests" cannot accurately measure strengths such as creativity, social skills, leadership, personal problem-solving, intuition, mechanical skills, artistic skills, sensitivity to others—all valuable attributes. Emphasize that they should never let any person or number "define" them and determine who they are.

6. For closure, ask for a volunteer to summarize the main point(s) of this session. Is there anything they might continue to think about in the days and weeks ahead? What were some feelings they had during the session?

focus: the self
should test scores define us?

background Conversation that centers on grades and test scores quickly becomes tedious and shallow—and competitive. Students with high ability need to be aware that such a preoccupation quickly loses its "coolness" after high school, and even in high school it usually smacks of arrogance and insensitivity to others. But students with high grades and test scores probably feel somewhat "defined" by them. The "system" has said they are "good."

Sometimes parents of gifted children become quite absorbed in their children's test scores and bring them up in social situations. Sometimes gifted children themselves get caught up in their test scores, comparing them with others' scores or feeling the need to use them for a frame of reference socially. This reinforces the feeling that one is "defined" by how one performs on tests.

Students whose grades and test scores are average or low are also "defined" by them. Many students do not function well in the school environment, and their grades usually reflect that. Their standardized achievement test scores might reflect the fact that they haven't absorbed some of the curriculum. The curriculum may be too challenging for them, or they may be in inappropriate classes. So the "system" sends a message to them that they are *not* "good." If they are known to have a high level of intelligence, they might be called "underachievers," so defined because of their grades—as compared with some measure of their ability and potential.

The more others emphasize test scores, the more students become preoccupied with them as "definers" in the competitive world of academics, scholarships, and college acceptances. However, test scores should never "define" a person, no matter what they may reveal about his or her intellectual or achievement potential. No single test can assess the broad range of traits and abilities that help to make a person successful and productive in society, a wonderful person to be around, or even a person of eminence. All tests are imperfect measurers.

Group ability test scores may be affected by any number of factors, including test anxiety, fatigue, stress, low verbal skills, learning disabilities, room temperature, attitude toward test-taking, cultural experiences, and cultural values that might not embrace competitiveness and test performance. A score on an *individually* administered ability test might also be affected by the gender and manner of the examiner. It may not reflect many strengths important to success in the real world.

However, test scores can be valuable indicators of who might benefit by special programs. They can raise a flag during the screening process and give the identifier reason to check out a student further. Great discrepancies among subtests might indicate potential for frustration and underachievement in the school system and can be used to determine where special help or curriculum modifications might be beneficial. Ability tests may find gifted individuals who otherwise would be missed because of poor grades. Achievement tests can identify individuals who are or are not absorbing the curriculum—or whose relatively low verbal abilities may be interfering with test-taking and academic achievement.

Then there are grades. Grades are often subjective and are sometimes capriciously or arbitrarily awarded. Teachers differ in stringency regarding grade-giving. Grading standards may differ from district to district, state to state, and certainly teacher to teacher. One written composition may receive widely differing grades from several English teachers. Some teachers reward creativity; some discourage it with low grades.

Tests and grades certainly have their place, and both are probably here to stay. But students should not be "defined" by either. This session can provide important information about the data that make up the "cumulative file" on every student. These data need to be kept in perspective.

objectives

- Students put grades and test scores into proper perspective.

- They learn that no test is a perfect measure of anything, that grades are not perfect representations of what a student has learned, and that the self should not be "defined" by either test scores or grades.

suggestions

1. Begin by asking the students how they feel about grades. If they need help getting started, ask questions like the following.

   ▶ What are grades for?

   ▶ If your school suddenly decided to stop giving grades, how would this affect your school performance?

   ▶ Do grades reflect what students really know?

   ▶ Do grades reflect what students have learned in a class? How intelligent they are? How conscientious they are? Their teacher-pleasing skills? Attendance? Class participation? Their understanding of the subject matter? Their problem-solving ability?

2. Find out how the students feel about standardized (normed on a representative national sample and taken nationally) achievement tests—the kind given annually or biennially, or the kind given to test college aptitude. Ask questions like the following.

   ▶ What are standardized achievement tests supposed to measure? (What has been learned in the curriculum.)

> What kinds of students do well on them? What kinds of students do poorly on them?

> What factors might affect a student's performance on a standardized achievement test?

> Female students often test less well than male students during high school. Can you think of any reason why this might happen? (Mention course selection as one possibility.)

> What abilities and skills do achievement tests *not* measure?

3. Initiate a discussion about intelligence and testing in general. You may find it helpful to read one or more of the following statements. Or pass them out on individual slips of paper and have students read them to the group.

> A person does not have to be "brilliant" to achieve very well in life. In fact, those who are "comfortably bright" can do just about anything if they have adequate motivation, perseverance, stability, and ability to "negotiate the system."

> No test can determine *how* one thinks.

> Working slowly on a test might not indicate a "slow mind." A student with high capability might, in fact, be evaluating thought processes. That student might also know more ways to consider the question than most people.

> Most tests rely heavily on verbal ability. A student's strengths might be in other areas.

> Intelligence tests do not measure creativity, leadership, ability to communicate, interpersonal sensitivity, everyday problem-solving ability, potential for success in life, or probability of success in the classroom. They also do not measure motivation and perseverance, which are important contributors to life success.

> Test anxiety, illness, the testing environment, and other factors can affect a student's scores on a particular test.

> No single test score can accurately or fairly "define" a particular student.

> Intelligence is not static. Although genetic factors play a role in determining intelligence, environment is key to its development.

4. Some theorists believe that intelligence is a *general* quality. Others believe there are different *kinds* of intelligence. In his book, *Frames of Mind: The Theory of Multiple Intelligences* (New York: Basic Books, 1983), Harvard psychologist Howard Gardner has identified seven intelligences. Share them with your group orally or write them on the chalkboard for all to see.

> Linguistic (sensitivity to oral and written language)

> Musical (composing; sensitivity to pitch, rhythm, tone, musical patterns)

55

▶ Logical-mathematical (science and math; ability to see patterns; ability to reason)

▶ Spatial (visual arts, engineering, chess; fascination with "shapes" in science—DNA model, organic compounds)

▶ Bodily-kinesthetic (athletics, dance, acting, inventing)

▶ Intrapersonal (understanding the self and being tuned into one's own "feeling" life)

▶ Interpersonal (ability to "read" people; leadership, diplomacy, politics, social skills).

Explain that standardized achievement tests mostly measure two kinds of intelligence: verbal and logical-mathematical. Most intelligence tests measure three kinds: verbal, logical-mathematical, and spatial. Grades usually reflect only a few of these intelligences. Other cultures might value other intelligences more highly than the ones that are usually tested for. For these and other reasons, we need to keep "intelligence" in perspective and appreciate that *many* abilities are important in a healthy society.

Referring to Gardner's model, ask the students which intelligence or intelligences they think they might be strong in, and which ones they think they might be weak in.

5. For closure, ask for summary comments about test scores and grades "defining" students. Tell them you hope this session has helped them to put tests and testing into better perspective.

focus: the self
understanding underachievement

background

Underachievement has been the subject of research for many decades, and it remains a complex phenomenon that stirs great debate. As many as 50 percent of highly capable students may not achieve well in school (Richert, 1991), and many students with high intelligence are not even recognized as such by their teachers.

For many students, home and school factors seem to interact to produce underachievement, and it can eventually become an entrenched "habit"—to the extent that it can become a lifestyle. Sometimes so much energy is siphoned off by responsibilities or conflict that there is little left for school-work. Perhaps, for other students, creativity or personality factors make them a poor fit in the school system. Some may suffer from depression.

Sometimes cooperation between school and home can contribute to improvement in a student's academic performance. Sometimes family counseling helps, with a look at what function the underachievement might serve within the family, how it affects various individuals, and what it might be a symptom of. Sometimes individual counseling about anger and control helps to deal with what might be passive-aggressive behavior on the part of the underachieving student.

Something that takes a long time to create, like underachievement, may take as long to change, and changing it should be seen as a process. Small, incremental improvements should be noticed and praised, such as *one* grade on *one* test in *one* course at a time.

Underachievers are the product of complex, interactive environments. It is unrealistic to hope or assume that a single discussion group session will have a significant impact on them. However, ongoing emphasis on self-awareness, family, relationships, and emotions often provokes positive change. A supportive group, with a supportive leader, can make a difference over the long term.

This session is a starting point, with an emphasis on some possible reasons for underachievement and some workable coping skills. Underachievers may learn something about themselves. Achievers may learn something about underachievement and become more sensitive to the problems of their underachieving classmates. Be sure to remind the students that many

57

successful adults had unsuccessful school experiences, and that those who achieve in school might not necessarily be as productive or satisfied later in life. The die is not necessarily cast during the school years.

Finally, if all or most of the students in your group are identified underachievers, you may want to divide this session into two. Your students may have a lot to say about underachievement, and it is worth taking the time to listen.

important

> **Throughout this session (or sessions, if you divide it into two), avoid any hint of preaching or judging. Quietly affirm the students' intelligence, worth, and dignity. Acknowledge that they are in control of their achievement. Avoid implying that they could do better if they tried. They have heard that before. Their grades may be all they feel they *can* control in their lives.**

reference

Richert, E. S. "Patterns of underachievement among gifted students." In Mireley, M., and Genshaft, J., eds., *Understanding the Gifted Adolescent.* (New York: Teachers College Press, 1991).

recommended resources

Heacox, Diane, *Up From Underachievement: How Teachers, Students, and Parents Can Work Together to Promote Student Success* (Minneapolis: Free Spirit Publishing, 1991). A step-by-step program to help underachievers break the failure chain and succeed in school. For all ages.

Rimm, Sylvia, *Underachievement Syndrome: Causes and Cures* (Watertown, WI: Apple Publishing Co., 1986). An analysis of various types of underachievers and a presentation of the TRIFOCAL model for treatment.

Whitmore, Joanne, *Giftedness, Conflict, and Underachievement* (Boston: Allyn and Bacon, 1980). A thorough treatment of underachievement, including research references.

objectives

- Students confront stereotypes of achievement and underachievement and re-think their own attitudes.

- Students become more aware of issues that affect motivation and achievement.

- Underachievers consider some possible strategies for functioning better in school.

suggestions

1. Introduce the topic with some ideas from the background information. Mention that many, many students with high capability do not achieve well in school. Although this may make the future difficult for them, it does not make success and satisfaction impossible. Underachievers need to figure out how to get what they need from "the system."

2. Ask the students to define "underachievement." If necessary, define it for them. You might say something like this: "Underachievement is generally defined as academic performance below what would be expected, based on some measure of ability. In other words, an underachiever may be a student who scores high on achievement or intelligence tests but does poorly in school."

3. Ask the group, "How do you think achievers usually feel about underachievers?" Allow for responses before asking, "And how do you think underachievers usually feel about achievers?" Afterward, ask, "Do you think achievers and underachievers have anything in common? Is each group stereotyped?" Discuss possible shared characteristics, such as feeling stress from expectations, sensitivity, family situations, social difficulties, and concern for the future.

4. Ask the group, "Do you think there are 'causes' of underachievement?" Mention that some or all of the following can be factors—*after* they have discussed their own view of contributing factors.

   moving from town to town, or from school to school

   death or illness within the family, or student illness

   emotional upheaval, including depression

   changing one's group of friends

   problems with siblings

   specific incidents that happen at school

   changes within the family

   parents' attitudes toward school

   role models

   changes in one's view of the world, or a world view that does not value academic achievement

   deciding that school isn't important or isn't challenging

   hostility toward parents and teachers

   wanting to take control of one's life

   Ask if any underachievers are willing to talk about when they began lower achievement. What was going on in their lives at the time?

5. Depending on the level of trust and honesty in the group and whether you think it is appropriate, ask the students to consider some or all of the following questions. Choose your questions carefully. Remember that one purpose of these discussion groups is to let students "just talk," so encourage your students to respond to these questions orally. However, if you have doubts about discussing these issues within the group, or if there are some questions you feel are invasive, feel free to create a written questionnaire with only a few selected questions.

   Achievers can respond to the general statements and, for most of the others, change "underachiever" to "achiever." Underachievers might be surprised by how achievers respond to the questions.

important

Respect any and all responses. Especially for the underachievers in your group, it is important that you listen as a caring adult, receiving their comments without challenging or criticizing them. It may be a novel experience for them to speak about feelings and be listened to without judgment.

▶ Where in your life are you letting your intelligence show?

▶ Who in your life believes that you are an intelligent person?

▶ Do you believe you are intelligent?

▶ How do you know you are intelligent?

▶ Do you think a lot? How often do you lie awake at night, thinking complex thoughts and trying to figure out complex situations?

▶ Do you have trouble concentrating?

▶ What is the most comfortable part of school for you? The most uncomfortable?

▶ Do you like to be aware of what's going on around you?

▶ How would you rate your "social savvy" or "street smarts"?

▶ What are your feelings about being labeled an "underachiever"?

▶ What would happen if you started achieving in school?

▶ How would various members of your family react if you started achieving in school?

▶ When you underachieve, who gives you attention?

▶ What do underachievers get out of underachieving? What makes it worthwhile to keep underachieving? (Ideas: attention from parents and teachers; peer acceptance; not being seen as a "brain;" being seen as a "rebel," not part of the system; not giving in to authority; distracting the family from worse issues.)

▶ Who are you being loyal to by underachieving?

▶ What are you sacrificing by underachieving?

▶ Do you feel you disagree with some part of the school system in general?

▶ How much are you in control of your school achievement (grades)?

▶ How much do you feel that you're in control of your future?

▶ Do you sometimes feel discouraged about life in general?

▶ What would help you feel better about yourself and your life?

▶ How much direction do you feel for your life right now?

▶ How confident are you that you could do well if you tried?

▶ How confident are you that you'll be able to handle college, if you choose to go to college and are accepted?

> ▶ How much influence do you have over the achievement of others in your peer group?

> ▶ How much do you brag about how little effort you make in school?

> ▶ How do you feel about competition?

> ▶ How much do you have trouble following rules and guidelines?

> ▶ Do you sometimes wonder if you have some sort of learning disability, or learning difference, that interferes with your ability to achieve in school?

6. Ask the students if they can think of any ways they could "use" the system to their advantage—in other words, get out of school what they need to succeed in life *without* sacrificing themselves to the system. Not all underachievers are rebels, but this kind of question sometimes raises new possibilities in the minds of underachieving students. Be aware that they might not yet be comfortable talking about actual changes they could make.

7. If all or most of the students in your group are identified under-achievers, and if they seem to have been comfortable and honest responding to the questions in suggestion #5, ask if they might be interested in trying an Underachievers Anonymous group for a few weeks. If they aren't interested, let it pass. If they are, continue.

   Hand out the "Underachievers Anonymous" activity sheet (page 62). Explain that each week they will write one small goal on their sheet. At the end of the week, they will use the sheet to report on their degree of success. Reassure the students that this will not take up a lot of group time, unless that is what they want and need. (As an alternative, the students participating in Underachievers Anonymous could meet separately to "check in.")

   Ask for student volunteers to read the statements at the top of the activity sheet. Make sure that everyone who will be participating in "UA" understands what is expected of them. (NOTE: You may want to keep a separate file folder for your Underachievers Anonymous group members. Explain that while it seems like a contradiction to have them write their names on their sheets, this is the only way you can keep them straight—unless you all agree on another method that works equally well.)

8. For closure, ask one or more students what new information, feelings, interaction, revelations, or awareness came out of the discussion.

underachievers anonymous (UA)

Name: _____

I will work conscientiously on the goals stated below as long as I am a member of the UA group.

I will check in weekly, assessing my progress, and stay committed to my goals.

I will refrain from bragging about any lack of effort, lateness, and/or any other underachieving behavior that implies that "the system" is beneath me.

I will try to remember that effort is the key to success, and I will try to give good effort to the work connected with these goals.

I understand the risks involved in this kind of commitment, but I believe they are worth it. I am doing this of my own free will, in my own self-interest.

I will try to keep in mind that all of this is good practice for adult life.

I will try to be supportive of others involved in UA, knowing that my attitudes and behaviors do influence others.

 WEEK   **GOAL**   **DEGREE OF SUCCESS IN REACHING MY GOAL**
(from 1 to 10, where 1 = no success and 10 = great success)

1. _____
2. _____
3. _____
4. _____
5. _____
6. _____
7. _____
8. _____
9. _____
10. _____

Signature: _____

focus: the self
giving ourselves permission

background Although all students could probably benefit from this session, it is geared especially to those whose high intelligence "interferes" with their being able to do and be what would be considered quite normal under most circumstances. You may want to introduce the session with a statement to that effect. Bright, capable people often censor, edit, constrain, inhibit, or "protect" themselves from various life experiences. They don't give themselves permission to say something that needs to be said, or to do something that might be beneficial (or interesting) to them.

This session works well with many age levels, as long as group members are capable of abstract thinking. I have used it with late elementary through college students and with adults. It feels relatively "safe," and participants can say as much or as little as they wish in reporting what they have checked on the activity sheet. It also moves any group ahead in open sharing, since it is quite thorough, and many aspects of a person are revealed in just a few moments. Finally, it is a potentially empowering exercise, since it clearly focuses on the individual's own power to grant (or not grant) permission to the self.

If your opportunity to lead a particular group is limited to only a few sessions, this should definitely be among them, since it promotes group bonding.

objectives
- Students recognize that they are in charge of how they respond to their various environments.
- They become aware that they could perhaps enhance their lives by giving themselves permission to do, say, or experience more.
- They learn that there are many common constraints that individuals place on themselves.
- They experience a sense of community within their group.

suggestions

1. Introduce the topic with whatever seems pertinent from the background information. Immediately hand out the "Giving Myself Permission" activity sheet (page 66). Explain that they may interpret each item however they wish.

   However, some students may not be accustomed to thinking of "being selfish" or "being angry" or "making mistakes" in anything but negative terms. You may want to point out that "being selfish" can mean taking care of important personal needs; "being angry" is better than "stuffing" anger and feeling hurt, sad, or frustrated; "making mistakes" is only human—and perfectly normal.

2. In this exercise, it is important for you to role model for the students. Read down your list, prefacing all or many of your items with the stem, "I would like to give myself permission to...," in order to impress on them that it would be possible for you to make a change if you had the requisite courage and will. Pause for a second or two after each item so that the group has a chance to register it. Throughout, it is important that you role model honesty and vulnerability.

3. Give the students a few minutes to complete their activity sheets; it should not take long. Remind them that they will mark what they *are not doing* at this point in their lives. Explain that the last item means "accept the fact that I sometimes have totally opposite feelings about a member of my family (like love/disgust, affection/irritation, approval/disapproval)." Tell them that they may add items to the list if something they want to give themselves permission to do is not included.

4. Encourage the students to share their lists. If you go around the circle, begin with a volunteer and then move in whatever direction will allow reluctant students to wait before sharing. As you modeled in suggestion #2, they should simply read down their lists, prefacing all or many of the items with "I would like to give myself permission to..." and pausing briefly between items. Encourage the group to listen carefully as each student shares his or her list.

   You may want to tally student responses in the margins of your own sheet. After everyone has finished sharing, you can then comment on or respond to specific items. It is also effective to end the session by reporting which items were checked most frequently.

5. After each person shares, ask the group if there is anything they would like to know more about, or if they heard anything that surprised them. For example, it's news if a star athlete wants to "feel good about my body," or if a high achiever wants to "be intelligent." If there is a dramatic insight or revelation, you might encourage the group to offer response and support. You may also want to ask for some elaboration. As always, each group member has the right to decline further comment.

64

6. Before closure, ask the students what items were reported most often. Verify their responses with your tally.

7. For closure, ask students to summarize the session. Ask one or more of the following questions, rhetorically, if you prefer.

    ‣ Did you find this session interesting?

    ‣ Did you gain any insights about yourselves or your age group?

    ‣ Were you surprised at anything?

    ‣ What one item from your list can you give yourself permission to start working on immediately—today?

giving myself permission

Name: _____

I would like to give myself permission to...

___ have fun	___ be free to "be" (independent of others' expectations)
___ take risks	___ accept authority in others
___ focus on the "now" instead of focusing so much on the future	___ live reasonably happily in an imperfect situation
___ be angry	___ be healthily and comfortably "alone"
___ be talkative	___ stop a bad behavior or a harmful habit
___ be quiet	___ be imperfect
___ be kind	___ relax
___ love	___ be "bad"
___ be loved	___ be "good"
___ feel good about my body	___ say difficult things to someone
___ be intelligent	___ take charge of my life
___ be selfish	___ affirm ambivalence about someone in my family
___ make mistakes	
___ achieve	___ _____
___ follow an independent course	___ _____
___ be outwardly upset	___ _____
___ be happy	
___ be sad	

focus: the self
what's in a name?

People often have strong feelings about their names. At certain ages and in certain situations, a name might seem "dumb" or embarrassing, not "masculine" or "feminine" enough, or too unique, common, old-fashioned, trendy, cute, young, long, or hard to pronounce. Perhaps it is too easily transformed into an unflattering nickname. Children whose names are difficult to pronounce may feel distressed or "anonymous" when their names are avoided or mispronounced.

What we think and feel about our names is affected by how others use them. Is our name often spoken in derision or with malice by someone whose opinion matters? Is it harmed by the reputation of a namesake? Is it spoken with respect? When people hear our name, do they associate it with good things or not-so-good things? This session may move in either light or very serious directions as group members share their feelings about their names.

objectives

- Students explore their feelings about their names.

- They articulate their feelings within the group and discover similarities.

- They are encouraged to feel proud of their names.

suggestions

1. Introduce the topic by saying that people usually have feelings about their names. Their feelings may change with age, but at some point (or points in time), a name may especially be a matter of scrutiny and sensitivity. Ask the students if they know the origins or meanings of their first or last names. They might share the ethnic roots of their names, if they know them. You might ask questions like the following.

   ▶ Do you know why you were given your first name or middle name?

   ▶ Do the names in your family have special significance in your family tree?

   ▶ Do you have a nickname? If so, where did it come from? Your family? The playground? A coach? A team?

67

2. If your group includes students from a variety of ethnic backgrounds, some with names that are difficult to pronounce, invite these students to teach their names to the group, and allow time for the group to practice saying them correctly. Don't allow the group to Anglicize or shorten a name. Instead, encourage them to concentrate on the student's real name out of respect. If the students choose, they may tell the group how they prefer to be addressed.

3. Ask, "Have you ever gone through a period when you didn't like your name—or when you liked it very much?" As various students share responses, ask questions like the following.

   ▶ Do you remember why you felt that way about your name? (Was it because of an association with someone in the news, in entertainment, or in athletics? Was the name "strange" or unusual, or too "common" and ordinary?)

   ▶ Have you ever been teased about your name, or has your name been used in a teasing way?

   ▶ Have your feelings about your name changed over the years? How have they changed? Why have they changed?

4. You might ask, "How do other people use your name? Do family members speak it with tenderness? Impatience? Love? Anger? Affection? How do people at school use it?"

5. If the members of your group are artistically inclined (or even if they aren't), distribute plain white paper and encourage them to write/draw their first names however they like, plain or fancy. Tell them to use drawings, cartoons, shading—anything that helps to communicate how they feel about their names. Afterward, have students show their names to the group. Invite them to explain why they chose to represent their names as they did.

6. For closure, tell the students that they are all good people with good names that deserve respect. Thank them for their contributions to the discussion.

focus: the self
time and priorities

objectives

- Students become more aware of the dominant American culture's preoccupation with time.
- They consider how this preoccupation affects them personally.
- They examine how they use their time outside of school.
- They assess their own ability to prioritize activities and use their time wisely.

suggestions

1. Start the session by asking the students to brainstorm all the compound words or phrases they can think of that include the word "time." Some examples follow.

saving time	taking time
making time	arranging a time
losing time	gaining time
overtime	time clock
time sheet	time-and-a-half
flex-time	part-time
full-time	leisure time
in time	on time
a reasonable time	in good time
high time	against time
time-share	timer
timekeeper	time-tested
standard time	daylight savings time
timetable	time to go
time out	time off
time's up	out of time

2. Offer the observation that language reflects what a culture emphasizes. Other cultures may not have so many words about "time"—or so many clocks.

3. Begin a discussion about time and how it affects our lives. Encourage the students to give specific examples of time constraints on their lives. What "price" do they pay? After they have shared, ask questions like the following.

  ▶ How does our preoccupation with time affect our ability to relax and enjoy life? Are you able to relax when you need to?

  ▶ Are we so caught up in instant gratification and quick fixes that we neglect or have trouble with things that take time? What about long-term relationships? Long-term projects? Reading long books or watching long movies? Learning new things that can't be learned overnight, such as a language? Are you involved in anything long-term?

  ▶ Have we accepted the idea that "more and faster" always equals "better"? Where might we see this in our society?

  ▶ Are we prisoners of time? Do our stress, fatigue, and frustration reflect that? Do we overextend ourselves? Do you feel "overextended"?

4. Invite the students to consider how their attitudes about time affect them personally. Ask, "What changes would you like to make in the way you perceive and use time? What would make you feel more satisfied with your life?" Encourage students to share their thoughts.

5. Introduce the concept of prioritizing activities. Hand out the "My Life Outside of School" activity sheet (page 71). Ask the students to divide the first "pie" into segments representing the average time they spend each week working, sleeping, eating, studying, socializing with friends, relaxing, and interacting with family.

6. Have the students present their pie charts and comment on whether they show "good prioritizing" or "poor prioritizing." Ask questions like the following.

  ▶ According to your pie chart, are you a good time manager?

  ▶ Are you spending enough (too much) time on your responsibilities? What about your needs? Your relationships?

  ▶ Are you spending too much time on one thing and not enough time on something else of equal or greater importance?

  ▶ What could you do to improve the way you spend your time?

  ▶ How do you *feel* about your time distribution?

  If time permits, tell the students that they may use the other "pie" on the activity sheet to show how they *would like* to spend their time. Discuss the differences between the first and second pie charts.

7. For closure, ask the students for their "timely" opinions about this session. Was it "time well spent"?

my life outside of school

Name: _____

Divide this "pie" into pieces showing how much time you spend each week working, sleeping, eating, studying, socializing with friends, relaxing, and interacting with family.

Divide this "pie" into pieces showing how you would like to spend your time.

focus: the self
in control, out of control

objectives

- Students consider the issue of control in their lives.
- They discuss what it means to be "in control" and "out of control."

suggestions

1. Introduce the topic by asking the students what comes to mind when they think about being "in control." They might mention the following.

academics	home life
social situations	conversation
leading a group	competition
athletics	music
relationships	

2. Now ask the students what they associate with being "out of control." Here they might mention some of the categories from suggestion #1 and others as well, perhaps including the following.

strong feelings	being around intimidating people
being "outclassed"	fears
depression	anxiety
abuse	having to abide by family rules
dating	food
conflict	anger
arguments	using alcohol and other drugs
being around members of the other gender	being in a group of peers doing something dangerous

   Common ground will probably emerge. Invite the students to share incidents from their lives when they felt "out of control." Share incidents from your life. You might say, "I feel comfortable sharing that. There are some other situations I wouldn't be comfortable sharing. Share whatever you are comfortable sharing." It is especially important to offer such guidance to young ages, although all ages seem to share discreetly, according to their level of trust.

3. Move the discussion toward what it means to have a sense of control in one's life. Ask questions like the following.

   ▶ What does it mean to have control in your life?

   ▶ To what extent do you feel that you have control in your life? Sometimes? Often? Always? A lot? A little?

   ▶ What do you think contributes to the feeling of having control in your life?

   ▶ Do you know anyone who seems to have control in life? Who? What makes you think this about him or her?

   ▶ What words would you use to describe that person? (Examples: cool, poised, unruffled, calm, strong, at ease, confident.)

   ▶ Are people who seem to be "in control" really "in control"?

   ▶ Do adults generally feel more "in control" than young students?

   ▶ Can a person be "in control" in a negative way? (Examples: controlling others, being abusive, using intimidation, manipulating.)

4. Invite the students to share what they hope will happen in their lives to give them a greater sense of control. They might also describe what they could do to gain more control. They might mention some of the following. Afterward, ask, "Do any of these things ensure 'control'?"

   counting to 10 before responding when angered

   relaxation techniques

   verbalizing feelings

   getting a good education

   being on their own

   having a good relationship

   getting or staying healthy

   getting a good job

   attaining financial security

   becoming an adult

5. For closure, ask a few or all students to describe what "being in control" means to them personally. Perhaps their thoughts and feelings changed in the course of the discussion.

focus: the self
assessing self-esteem

An important task for adolescents is to develop a personal identity—to find out who they are. To do this, they may try on various images and check out the responses of peers, parents, and teachers. They may become self-critical, gauge their worth by measuring themselves against the standards set by their peer culture, dream impossible dreams, or identify with superheroes. When they do not measure up—when they make mistakes, are embarrassed, or feel "different"—their self-esteem suffers.

Many adolescents do not express their lack of confidence and their doubts about themselves. Many (perhaps most) do not seek out trusted adults to talk to. This session can give students a chance to talk about what they think of themselves in a safe and supportive group of peers, who are always listened to more intently than adults.

All adolescents wrestle with self-esteem to some extent, even (sometimes especially) students with high ability. If all or most of the students in your group are gifted, do not assume that they are less concerned than other students about identity and acceptance. Hormonal shifts and volatile emotions may make them feel "out of control"—for perhaps the first time in their lives. Their old coping strategies may no longer work for them. Suddenly social ease is paramount—and elusive. They may feel out of step. They may be dealing with the pain of being different. Perhaps they would rather not join the adolescent focus on competitive fashion, but feel they must. They may not be as adept socially as they are intellectually. The pressures continue for success, which may not come as easily as it has in the past.

Low self-esteem has a ripple effect in a young life. It affects relationships with peers and family. It plays a role in a number of behaviors, from shyness and poor classroom participation to cruel gossiping, bullying, and intimidation of peers and siblings. It can contribute to vulnerability to abuse in relationships, as well as to alcohol and drug abuse and other dangerous and self-destructive behaviors. Even the most apparently "successful" students may be suffering from low self-esteem. They, too, may be plagued by fears and doubts. The high-achieving student with seemingly cool composure may be struggling to maintain control in a chaotic family situation.

We can seldom tell by appearances alone if our students "know who they are" and what they think of themselves. Whether your group is all successful achievers, all potential drop-outs, or a combination of both, you can be sure that the need to articulate self-esteem problems is there.

important

It's best to place this session far enough into the group experience that positive comments have credibility. When such comments are made early in the life of the group, they may not be believed, since "that person doesn't know me well enough to say those things about me."

objectives

- Students assess their own self-images in a supportive group setting.
- They consider the sources of self-esteem.
- They become aware that low self-esteem can negatively affect life as an adult.
- They brainstorm ways to improve their self-esteem.
- They practice giving and receiving self-esteem-enhancing comments.

suggestions

1. Introduce the topic by handing out the "Rating My Self-Esteem" activity sheet (page 78). Give the students a few minutes to complete their sheets.

2. Have the students tell how they arrived at their self-esteem ratings. Ask questions like the following.

    ▶ What contributed to your (physical, intellectual, social, emotional) self-esteem rating?

    ▶ What messages have been sent to your self by family and friends?

    ▶ What personal standards have you set for yourself (physically, intellectually, socially, emotionally)?

    ▶ What are the (physical, intellectual, social, emotional) standards of your peer group?

    ▶ What are your family's (physical, intellectual, social, emotional) standards?

3. Invite the students to consider where self-esteem comes from. Ask questions like the following.

    ▶ Is self-esteem "given" to us through praise, gifts, and attention? Or does it come from within?

    ▶ Do we have a choice in how we respond to others' messages?

    ▶ How do we develop self-esteem? (If the students don't mention the following, contribute them to the discussion: learning how to do things for ourselves; learning how to be responsible; gaining skills through meeting challenges.)

> ▶ Are self-esteem and self-sufficiency the same?

> ▶ What kind of parenting encourages children to develop self-esteem?

> ▶ How do you know you're okay? How do you know you're valued? (Be aware that some students may indicate that they do *not* know they are valued. If that occurs, encourage the group to offer support—especially if they have previously demonstrated that capacity.)

4. Ask, "What parts of adult life might be affected by low self-esteem, and how?" Introduce the following ideas if they do not come up in discussion.

> ▶ marriage (feelings of inadequacy; being abused or abusive; being unhealthily competitive or critical)

> ▶ parenting (feelings of inadequacy; being abused or abusive; inability to be close to one's children; alienation; rigidity; fearfulness; isolation; pessimism)

> ▶ social relationships (feelings of inadequacy; tendency to dominate others or be dominated by them)

> ▶ relationships at work (inability to compliment and support others; gossiping; being non-assertive)

> ▶ career direction and success (feelings of inadequacy; inability to make necessary career moves; lack of focus)

> ▶ productivity (preoccupation with one's flaws and inadequacies; lack of a "can-do" attitude)

> ▶ contentment and satisfaction with life (low or nonexistent)

5. Have the students brainstorm ways to start improving their self-esteem *now*. Following are some suggestions.

> ▶ Give yourself compliments and praise instead of relying on others to do it.

> ▶ When it comes, receive and accept approval instead of rejecting it.

> ▶ "Parent" yourself. Do for yourself what others have been unable to do for you. (This is especially important for teenagers who have grown up in chaotic, depressed, abusive, or alcoholic homes, where parents may not have been able to "parent.")

> ▶ Do something you know you're good at, and then congratulate yourself for a job well done.

> ▶ Try something new. Even if you "fail," congratulate yourself for being brave enough to take the risk.

> ▶ Accept and acknowledge all of your feelings, even the "bad" ones: anger, guilt, inadequacy, disappointment.

6. Ask the students to write down at least one positive comment about everyone in the group (including themselves). Then, focusing on one student at a time, have everyone share their positive comments about that student. Given probable time constraints, you will have to move this activity along fairly quickly. Let the comments stand alone; give them time to be heard, but do not discuss them. You might suggest that each student wait to hear all comments from the group before saying a simple, "Thank you."

7. For closure, thank the group for sharing, for articulating their concerns in sensitive areas, and for being generous and thoughtful in their comments.

rating my self-esteem

Name: _____

Rate your own self-esteem, on a scale of 1 (very low) to 10 (very high), in each of the following four areas:

PHYSICAL

1   10
_____

INTELLECTUAL

1   10
_____

SOCIAL

1   10
_____

EMOTIONAL

1   10
_____

Now give yourself a general self-esteem rating:

1   10
_____

focus: the self
making mistakes

objectives

- Students share their feelings about making mistakes.
- They hear the message that making mistakes is only human.

suggestions

1. As soon as all of the students have arrived and are seated, say: "Close your eyes and think about the last significant mistake you made in the presence of at least one other person . . . Imagine the scene . . . You have just made the mistake . . . Who is there with you? . . . What are you feeling? . . . Are you expecting someone to say something to you about the mistake? . . . Does this happen? . . . What else happens? . . . What is your response—to the other person's comment, or to the silence? . . . How do you feel? . . . How long does this feeling last?"

2. Share a related experience from your own life—a time when you made a mistake, someone said something about it (or not), and how you felt about it. Then encourage the students to share their experiences. Let them respond to and support one another, perhaps adding comments about similar experiences.

3. Afterward, ask the group how they felt during the exchange. (Relaxed? Apprehensive? Close to one another? Embarrassed? Uneasy?) Ask questions like the following.

   ▶ How did it feel to share your "imperfect" side?

   ▶ How would you describe the "atmosphere" during the sharing? Did it seem honest? Supportive?

   ▶ Did your sharing make a contribution?

   ▶ How might your sharing have an effect on the group?

   ▶ Did sharing "mistakes" change your views of each other?

4. Initiate a general discussion about mistakes, the students' experience with making mistakes, and the consequences of their mistakes. Ask questions like the following.

   ▶ How do you usually feel about your mistakes?

▶ Is there someone in your life who seems to enjoy pointing out your mistakes or "pouncing" on them? Do you spend a lot of time around this person?

▶ What happens at home when you make a mistake?

▶ What happens when you make a mistake around your friends?

▶ What might happen if someone tried to avoid making mistakes at all costs?

▶ What is a healthy attitude about making mistakes, in your opinion?

5. For closure, invite the group to create a motto or maxim about mistakes. If they seem stuck, offer examples, perhaps including "I have the right to make mistakes," "Nobody's perfect," and/or "Mistakes are only human." Thank the students for sharing their personal experiences.

focus: the self

do heroes and heroines reflect values?

- Students think about whether they have heroes/heroines.
- They consider whether the heroes/heroines of today are different from heroes/heroines of the past.
- They consider whether their heroes/heroines reflect their personal values.

1. Introduce the topic with the following observation (in these words or your own): "Some people believe that young people today—unlike young people of the past—don't have heroes/heroines. Or, if they do, their heroes/heroines are poor role models. I don't know what the word 'hero'/'heroine' means to you. Is it someone who inspires you or serves as a role model for you? Is it someone who has accomplished something you admire, embodies values and virtues you admire, has helped you personally, or has overcome some problem or adversity? Your heroes/heroines (if you have them) may be real or fictional, young or old, living or dead. Write a list of your heroes/heroines. If you don't have any heroes/heroines, list people you respect or admire. If you can't think of any heroes/heroines—or any people you respect or admire—write 'none.'"

    Or, as an alternative to this introduction, simply ask the students to list their heroes/heroines without giving any suggestions about how to interpret the word.

2. Encourage the students to share their lists. Ask them to pause briefly between the names on their lists so that others have a chance to think about them. If they like, they may tell why they listed each one in turn, or they might wait until they have read through their lists and then comment generally on their reasons for listing those individuals.

3. When all students have read their lists, ask the students to point out any similarities in their lists. Perhaps many students named one or more of the same people as heroes/heroines. Or perhaps the heroes/heroines they listed have characteristics or traits in common.

4. Generate discussion with questions like the following.

> ▸ Have your heroes/heroines changed over time?

> ▸ Did you have different heroes/heroines when you were younger? Or have some of your heroes/heroines stayed the same for many years?

> ▸ Have all of your heroes/heroines had similar traits? Do they represent your values?

> ▸ (For those who wrote "none" on their lists): Was there a time when you did have heroes/heroines?

5. Invite students to comment on whether their heroes/heroines embody traits they have themselves or wish they had.

6. If you introduced the session with the observation in suggestion #1, ask, "Do young people today have different heroes/heroines than their parents or grandparents did?" If several students in the group wrote "none" on their lists, ask, "Do you think you're typical of people your age in having no heroes/heroines?"

7. For closure, ask the students, "If, in fact, heroes/heroines reflect personal values, what might you say about the values of the group, judging by the heroes/heroines that were listed?" Then, "Are the values of the group similar to the values of most people your age today?"

focus: the self
having fun

background

Although this topic may seem inappropriate for a discussion group setting, and although most of your students may already seem to know plenty about having fun, it merits attention.

Some students socialize a great deal without "having fun." Some have parents who send the message that "having fun" is not appropriate in school—or in life. Some may appear to be having fun, but in fact are envious of those who *really* seem to be enjoying life.

High-achieving students may not take time to relax and have fun—and may not know where to start to do either. Gifted underachievers may be similarly unable to "enjoy the moment." Some may be too angry or frustrated to have fun. Some might be too depressed even to *imagine* fun. Some may translate "having fun" into dangerous, harmful, destructive, or self-destructive behaviors.

This session brings a seemingly "light" topic forward for serious discussion. In this stressful age and society, everyone needs to talk about fun—and learn how to have it.

objectives

- Students learn that having fun is part of a healthy, balanced life.
- They become more aware of whether and how they have fun.
- They brainstorm ways to have "creative fun."
- They recognize that it is possible to have fun as an adult—even at work.

suggestions

1. Begin by having the students define the word "fun." What does it mean to them? Accept their responses without comment.
2. Encourage them to share what they normally do for fun. Where do they go? Who are they with? How long do they spend on their chosen activity?

3. Initiate a discussion about fun in general. Ask questions like the following.

   ▶ Do you make sure to include fun and relaxation in your life?

   ▶ Do you set aside part of each day for fun and relaxation? How do you manage that?

   ▶ How easy is it to find time for fun and relaxation?

   ▶ Do you feel any pressure *not* to have fun? Where does this pressure come from? Is it internal (from you) or external (from others)?

   ▶ How satisfied, happy, and relaxed do you feel after doing whatever you do to have fun?

   ▶ How did you learn to have fun? Who has modeled "having fun" for you?

   ▶ Do your parents have fun?

   ▶ Do you feel that you need more fun in your life?

   ▶ Are the things you do for fun ever unhealthy, destructive, or dangerous?

   ▶ Are you often restless and bored, with nothing to do?

4. Introduce the concept of "creative" fun. (This is especially important if some students in your group are into unhealthy, destructive, or dangerous "fun" activities, or if many students complain about being bored and having nothing to do.) Invite the students to brainstorm ideas for fun activities that meet the following criteria.

   ▶ It's something I can do with a friend or in a group. People interact.

   ▶ It promotes communication. People talk and laugh together.

   ▶ It doesn't hurt anyone, including me.

   ▶ It helps people get to know each other better, maybe even become friends.

   ▶ It doesn't involve alcohol or other drugs.

   ▶ It brings out the best in everyone involved.

5. Make the connection between having fun and being childlike. You might say something like this: "Some people think that having fun is 'just for kids.' Think of things you did as a child that were fun for you. Is there anything from your past that you're still doing for enjoyment today? Is there anything from your past that you'd like to be doing today, as a teenager? How could you translate this into an activity that's appropriate for your age group?"

6. Invite the students to look ahead to fun in their future. Ask questions like the following.

> ▶ Is it okay for adults to have fun?

> ▶ Is it okay for work to be fun? Do you know anyone for whom work seems like play? Someone who derives a lot of enjoyment from his or her job?

> ▶ How do the adults you know have fun—if they have fun?

> ▶ When you picture yourself as an adult having fun, what do you see yourself doing? (NOTE: Encourage the students to imagine activities other than drinking, if their responses are mostly centered around alcohol.)

> ▶ When you're an adult, how will you ensure a balance between work and play in your life?

7. For closure, either summarize the session yourself or ask the students to tell what they have heard from the group. Commend them for taking this subject seriously, and wish for them balanced lives that include fun, relaxation, and laughter.

focus: the self
each of us is an interesting story

background

This session can be a meaningful experience for all students. It can help them to sort the various strands or "threads" in their personal history, affirm the richness of their lives, and appreciate that all of life's experiences—pleasant or painful, delightful or difficult—combine to make us remarkable and interesting. The incidents in our lives give us wisdom, strength, resiliency, vision, compassion, and complex emotions.

No one is bland or boring. Everyone's story is complex and full of "texture." Each of us is unique. Our life stories are like handmade quilts—original, colorful, one-of-a-kind. Whatever metaphor you choose (or your students suggest), the idea that each of us is an interesting story can begin to cast a positive light on all life situations, including those that are challenging or difficult.

Since the "My Story" activity requires at least ten minutes to prepare, and each student in the group should get the group's full attention when presenting his or her story, you may want to divide this session in two, depending on the time available. *Be sure to collect the activity sheets after the first session for use during the following session.*

objectives

- Students learn that each of them is a "story" that is worth recording, hearing, learning about, and learning from.

- They experience that sharing parts of their personal story helps to build bridges to others and forges bonds of friendship and support.

suggestions

1. Introduce the topic with some ideas from the background information above. Hand out the "My Story" two-page activity sheet (pages 88–89). Tell the students that they will spend part of today's session completing it. Instruct them to look at the various parts of the activity sheet as you read through the following guidelines.

   ▶ Treat your life as a story. Pretend that you're a novelist or are writing your autobiography.

   ▶ Don't worry about writing complete sentences. Brief notes are okay. This isn't English class, and your story won't be graded.

> ◗ Be clever and creative, and use humor if you like, but please take this activity seriously.

> ◗ For #2, "Chapter Titles," it might help if you divide your life story into chronological periods, important family events, major changes, or whatever suits you.

> ◗ For #3, try to think of themes you remember from studying literature. (Examples: "winning is everything," "survival against the odds," "change is the only certainty.")

Ask if anyone has questions about any other part of the "My Story" activity sheet. Respond to questions. Then allow at least 10 minutes for students to complete their sheets. They can add items as they listen to others later. Be aware that some may finish quickly, and some may want time to write many details.

2. Invite the students to share their stories one at a time. Tell them that they may share all or part of what they have written, elaborating or omitting according to what seems appropriate and comfortable to them. Instruct the group to listen for other themes that emerge, beyond those requested in #3 and #12 on the "My Story" sheet.

3. If students share difficult situations, experiences, or facts, or if anyone becomes distressed while sharing or listening, offer support and encourage the group to do likewise. Remind the students that all parts of a person's life are important and that all contribute to the complexity of the whole person. Affirm all experiences—pleasant and unpleasant, positive and negative.

4. For closure, thank them for their stories. Affirm their rich, complex, varied, and interesting lives. Celebrate their uniqueness as individuals.

my story

Name: _____

1. Title: _____

2. Chapter titles:

   Chapter One: _____

   Chapter Two: _____

   Chapter Three: _____

   Chapter Four: _____

   Chapter Five: _____

   _____

   _____

   _____

3. Basic themes:

   a. _____

   b. _____

   c. _____

4. Villains/adversaries/enemies/"evil ones":

   _____

   _____

5. Heroes/heroines/saints/angels/benefactors:

   _____

   _____

6. What/who shaped me:

   _____

   _____

7. Turning points:

   _____

   _____

my story continued

8. Very dramatic scenes:

_____

_____

9. Chapters with great description—because I recall how everything looked:

_____

_____

_____

10. Very clear and powerful memories:

_____

_____

_____

11. "Blank" periods in my life—I can't remember much about them:

_____

_____

12. Repeating personal patterns in my life story:

_____

_____

13. The villains are punished by: _____

14. The heroes/heroines are rewarded by: _____

15. The most compassionate, most understanding character in my life story:

_____

16. The "good neighbor":

_____

17. The "best friend":

_____

18. The "healer":

_____

19. A leader/mentor/guide:

_____

20. A possible sequel to this story will tell about:

_____

focus: the self
when we need courage

This session gives group members an opportunity to share an incident from their lives that required courage. Confronted with danger, physical or psychological, they found the strength they needed to face it, even if they were afraid. They may not have realized at the time that they were being courageous, perhaps because they were preoccupied with the situation and were concentrating on surviving or moving past the crisis. Now, looking back, they can affirm the strength they demonstrated.

This is an especially positive experience for adolescents, who may feel that most of the events in their lives are largely beyond their control, or even that they are victims.

objectives

- Students recall times when they were courageous.
- They recognize that courage is needed for honest self-assessment, as well as for times when they are faced with a danger or threat.

suggestions

1. Introduce the topic with ideas from the background information above. Ask the students to think of times when they needed courage to face a threat, danger, or difficulty in their lives. If they need help, ask questions like the following.

   ▶ Has there ever been a time when your family was in danger because of problems within the family or threats from outside of the family? (Examples: a family crisis, a serious illness or accident, parents on the verge of divorce, the loss of a job, financial problems, a natural disaster.) Did your family find the courage to survive the dangerous period?

   ▶ Has there ever been a time when you had to confront someone you were afraid of or were intimidated by? (Examples: a bully, someone who threatened you or a sibling, someone with a reputation for violent behavior.)

   ▶ Has there ever been a time when you faced a danger or threat alone—and survived?

   ▶ Have you ever been in a physically dangerous situation?

◗ Were you ever caring for a child who suddenly needed help or protection?

◗ Have you ever had to stand up against peer pressure in a difficult situation?

◗ Have you ever had to stand up to a parent or other adult when it took great courage to do so?

◗ Can you remember a time when it would have been easy to avoid doing something difficult, but you found the courage to get it done?

2. Share an example of a time in your own life when you were courageous. Encourage the students to share their examples. Allow time for students to tell their stories and for the group to respond. Encourage positive, affirming responses. Afterward, ask, "How did it feel to recall times when you were courageous? How does it feel to know that you had the strength to face a difficult situation?"

3. Turn the discussion to the relationship between courage and self-assessment. If time permits, ask questions like the following.

◗ You've just told about times when you were courageous in the face of danger or a threat. Does it take more courage, or less, to look honestly at yourself? Can you think of an example when you have done that?

◗ Does it take more courage, or less, to admit your mistakes? To take responsibility for your actions? To accept the consequences? Can you think of an example from your life?

◗ Does it take courage to make big changes in your life? What about getting out of a relationship that isn't good for you, even if it means being alone? Have you ever made a courageous change?

◗ Does it take courage to be honest about your feelings, especially when they are unpleasant or unpopular? Can you think of a time when you faced such feelings?

◗ Does it take courage to put the past behind you—to leave old memories behind—and get on with your life in the present? Have you ever done that?

◗ Does it take courage to be justifiably and appropriately angry at someone who has harmed you in some way—and to let that person know you are angry? Can you think of an example from your life?

4. Ask if anyone in the group is in need of courage right now or will be in the near future. If one or more students choose to share a crisis, problem, or situation that requires courage, listen supportively and encourage the other group members to show support. Remind the group of the need for confidentiality; some students may share sensitive information.

5. For closure, commend the students for the courage they showed in the past—and in the present, by sharing their stories with the group. You might also say something like this: "You probably know each other better now than you did at the beginning of this session. That happens when people share some of themselves, as we did today."

focus: the self
a prisoner of image

Per Hansa, the sturdy pioneer who is the main character in O. E. Rolvaag's novel *Giants in the Earth*, is greatly respected by his neighbors. He embodies the frontier spirit, and he meets the challenges of locusts, harsh winters, capricious weather, famine, scarce fuel, and a depressed wife with determination and courage. Near the end of Rolvaag's classic saga of immigrant life on the Midwestern prairie, Per Hansa's best friend is dying from pneumonia as a fierce blizzard rages outside. Friend Hans Olsa begs Per Hansa to go for help, and the others, too, say he must go. Hans's wife says, "We all have a feeling that nothing is ever impossible for you . . . ." And so he goes, against all reason. Later, he is found frozen by a haystack.

Per Hansa had an image as someone who could—and would—do the impossible. He felt obliged to live up to his image and meet his friends' expectations, despite his own better judgment. Although most image problems don't have such dire results, adolescents can probably identify with Per Hansa's problem. They, too, may have difficulty breaking free of an image others have of them—even when health and happiness may be at stake.

The teenager who is labeled "rebel," "risk-taker," "joker," or "social" may feel stuck in that role. The "bubbly," "buoyant, "energetic" student may feel constrained from expressing sadness. "Mr. Nice Guy" may be tired of being nice. The class comedian may yearn to be taken seriously. The "brain" may wish to ask a "stupid question," but may not feel allowed to do so.

It is possible to be a prisoner of one's image, so that no other behavior seems acceptable. It takes courage *not* to do what's expected of us. For the student burdened with a bad image—"druggie," "drunk," "promiscuous"—it can be especially difficult to escape.

objectives

- Students consider the image other people have of them.
- They consider the price they pay for living up to an image.
- They imagine what would happen if they didn't live up to their image.

suggestions

1. Introduce the topic by asking the students, rhetorically, "What's your image? How do other people see you?" If necessary, mention some of the images from the background information above. (Save the Per Hansa example for suggestion #2.)

2. Tell them about Per Hansa or give an example from your own life experience. Use the example to point out how one can be imprisoned by an image.

3. Ask the students to think of times in their own lives when they had an image to live up to. If they need help, read aloud some of the images from the list that follows. Ask, "Can anyone identify with these? What has been your unique, perhaps burdensome image?"

    class clown
    underachiever
    anti-school
    cynical
    Straight-A student/honor roll student
    winner
    loser
    someone who can handle anything
    cool
    in control
    good girl/boy
    bad girl/boy

    As students start revealing their images, ask questions like the following.

    ▶ What might you sacrifice or lose if you always live up to your image?

    ▶ What might happen if you didn't live up to your image? Would you lose respect? Identity?

    ▶ Has your image ever caused problems for you?

    ▶ How do you feel about other people who behave in ways that don't fit their image? Does this make them more or less interesting to you?

4. Ask the students if they would like to know what other people see as their "image." If some or all are willing to find out, continue. For each student who volunteers, have the other students describe what they believe that student's image to be. Then ask the student, "How did it feel to hear how others see you? Are they accurate? Does your image limit you in any way? Can you live up to your image?"

5. For closure, ask for a volunteer to summarize the session. What about it was thought-provoking?

94

focus: the self
feeling free

- Students think about the meaning of personal freedom.
- They consider what contributes to feeling free.

NOTE: If your time is very limited, you may want to begin with suggestion #4.

1. Begin by inviting the students to think of people who seem to be "free." These should be people they know personally—friends, relatives, children, adults. Ask the students to describe these people to the group. (Naming names is probably acceptable here because it is done in a positive way.) Have them explain why they see each person as being "free" and what "freedom" means in each case.

   This part of the discussion may move far away from the concept of personal freedom. Let it find its own course. Your group will likely express important feelings and thoughts, and this should always be a goal of each session. As students offer new individuals, their definition of "freedom" might even change.

2. Invite the students to think about what they just heard. Ask questions like the following to stimulate discussion.

   - What is the age of most of the people you named? Are most of them adults? Peers? Family members?

   - Are they married? Single? Intelligent? Educated? At peace with themselves? Active? Passive? Aggressive? Assertive?

   - Are they involved? Uninvolved? Living with rules? Living without rules? Making a contribution? Destructive to society?

   - If they are peers, are they living with their parents? Living on their own? Successful at something? Unconcerned with success? Financially secure? Not concerned with money?

   Finally, ask the group what conclusions they can draw about "freedom" and "feeling free," based on the discussion so far. If they can handle abstract discussions, ask them if guidelines and rules help or hinder "freedom." Do they get in our way or give us clear limits to be "free" within?

3. Turn the focus on the students themselves with questions like the following.

   ▶ Do you feel "free"?

   ▶ If you do, how does that feel?

   ▶ If you don't, how does that feel?

   ▶ If you don't feel free, what would help you to feel more free? Does "freedom" equal the ability to make choices?

4. If time allows, hand out the "Freedom of Choice" activity sheet (page 97) and ask the students to complete it. Share your own responses, and then encourage group members to share theirs.

5. For closure, emphasize the points made in items 7 through 10 on the "Freedom of Choice" activity sheet. Then ask the students to summarize the session. Wish for them good choices in life as they exercise their freedom to choose.

freedom of choice

Name: _____

1. I can't _____
   I can't _____
2. I won't _____
   I won't _____
3. If I could _____,
   I would.
4. In my life, I'm in charge of _____
   _____
5. I'm not in charge of _____
   _____
6. When _____
   and _____,
   I'll probably feel more free.
7. These are the choices I've made lately that show I have the freedom to choose in my life:
   _____
   _____
   _____
8. This is what I've done lately that shows I take responsibility for my choices:
   _____
   _____
   _____
9. These are times when I have allowed others to make choices for me:
   _____
   _____
   _____
10. What does "choice" have to do with "freedom"? Are we "free" even if we make no choices?
   _____
   _____
   _____

focus: the self
daydreaming

- Students share their dreams about the future.
- They discover that *everyone* daydreams in school.
- They explore how daydreaming can be both helpful and harmful.

1. Describe for the group the circumstances in which you are most likely to daydream. Invite the students to share similar information about themselves. (This starts them thinking about the topic without getting defensive about it.) Ask, "When do you daydream? Where? About what? Do you have a favorite daydream—one you return to again and again?"

2. Invite the students to project into the future by saying: "Close your eyes and project yourself into the future... You are now 30 to 35 years old . . . Think about your lifestyle . . . what kind of job you have . . . what you look like . . . the people you live with . . . where you live (a city? a town? the country? a house? an apartment?) . . . the things you enjoy doing . . . ."

   Afterward, encourage the students to share the images that came to mind.

3. Ask the students if they ever daydream in school. If your group consists of students with mixed abilities or mixed achievement levels, they may be surprised to learn that they all do. Take a few moments to explore this further with questions like the following.

   ▶ Why do you daydream in school? (High achievers may respond that they daydream when things are going too slowly for them. Underachievers may answer that daydreaming is more interesting than what's happening in class. Some students may say that they daydream when they don't understand what's happening in class.)

   ▶ Where do you "go" when you daydream?

   ▶ Does daydreaming help you to "cope"?

4. Explore both the positive and the negative sides of daydreaming with questions like the following.

   ▶ Can people daydream too much? How much is "too much"?

   ▶ Have you ever been in trouble for daydreaming in school? At home?

   ▶ Is it normal to daydream? How do you know?

   ▶ Is it possible to get good ideas from daydreaming?

   Invite the students to share some of the good ideas they have had while daydreaming. Ask them if they have ever acted on these ideas.

5. For closure, ask the students to complete this sentence: "Daydreaming is . . . ."

focus: the self
taking stock

This topic can be thought-provoking for any age and ability level. Students at risk need a chance to assess where they are on the growing-up continuum. High-achieving students appreciate having a safe place to express their doubts and fears about themselves and their future. Any adolescent can benefit from self-assessment in the presence of supportive peers and a caring adult.

Especially when life seems chaotic and unsettled, or when confusion exists about identity and direction, it is good to pause and "take stock." It is also good to experience others doing the same.

objectives

- Students gain self-awareness through taking stock of themselves at this interesting point in their lives.

- They put their past, present, and future into perspective.

suggestions

1. Introduce the topic with your own thoughts about "taking stock." Do you do this periodically? Is it beneficial to you? When and why do you "take stock"? (Make sure the students understand what you mean by "taking stock." If necessary, define it for them in general terms: examining your life, reviewing where you came from, considering where you are now, and thinking ahead to where you want to be in the future.)

2. Hand out the "I Am..." activity sheet (page 102). Ask the students to complete the "I Am..." statement with nouns, adjectives, or phrases that describe who they are. Instruct them *not* to include their hobbies, favorite courses, favorite foods, favorite colors, pets, or anything else that usually appears on a data list. If your group has difficulty getting started, share your own "I Am" list or another example like the following.

   I am...

...a female	...a lover of books
...an oldest daughter	...a second child
...a friend of many	...a procrastinator

...a weird thinker   ...a creative manipulator

...an unserious student   ...a messy housekeeper

Tell them to ignore the questions at the bottom of the sheet for now.

3. When the students have completed the "I Am..." section of the activity sheet, instruct them to answer the questions at the bottom: "Where have I been?" and "Where am I heading?" Give guidance appropriate to the group's abstract-thinking abilities. You might ask questions like the following.

   ▶ Have you been through the pits, and are you heading into happiness?

   ▶ Have you been through a bumpy (happy, chaotic, crazy) childhood and are heading into an equally bumpy (happy, chaotic, crazy) future?

   ▶ Have you been through many unsatisfying relationships and are now heading into more of the same?

   ▶ Have you been secure and happy in the past and are now heading in a less secure direction?

   ▶ Have you been through a period where you knew where you were going and are now heading into a time of less certainty?

   ▶ Have you been confused and are you heading into a period of less confusion?

4. If time permits, have the students assess how they are different now from how they were a year ago.

5. For closure, commend the group for their interesting, thoughtful lists and responses. Encourage them to continue "taking stock" of themselves periodically in order to keep discovering who they are. It is usually hard to be what we are not. Perhaps we can be who we are more comfortably when we know who that is.

i am . . .

Name: _____

List nouns, adjectives, or phrases that describe who you are. Complete this section before answering the questions at the bottom of the page.

_____

_____

_____

_____

_____

_____

_____

_____

_____

_____

Where have I been?

_____

_____

_____

_____

_____

Where am I heading?

_____

_____

_____

_____

_____

_____

focus: the self

a question of values: what matters to me?

background

We hear a lot about "values" today—"values education," "family values," "personal values." Generally speaking, values are the "rules" of a culture or society. Synonyms include "beliefs," "code," "doctrine," "ethics," and "philosophy."

Values are often the focus of controversy because people interpret and apply them in different ways. One person's "family values" may be perceived by another as old-fashioned and out of step. Some people do not identify with the values of their society. One culture's values may include disregarding or even destroying another culture's values.

Is it true that our values are changing? Who passes our values on? Is the family responsible for this task? Given the fact that so many families are breaking up and breaking down, can we still expect them to perform this vital function? Can unhealthy families pass on healthy family values? Is conscientious parenting becoming a lost value?

Depending on your group, you may use this session to openly address these and other important questions about values and what they mean in our lives. You might simply let students assess their own values and compare them to the values held by their parents, without drawing broad conclusions.

objectives

- Students consider the values that are important to them and their families.
- They note the differences and similarities between their values and those of their parents.
- They examine their values in light of their plans for the future.
- They learn about the values of the other group members.

suggestions

1. Hand out the two-page activity sheet, "A Question of Values" (pages 105–106). Have the students complete the activity. Explain that it involves identifying possible "values" that will probably help to guide their adult lives. Their "values" reflect what is important to them.

If they feel that don't know enough about their parents' values, they might concentrate only on "self."

2. Encourage the students to share their responses by "polling" the group. Ask, for example, "How many of you marked 'service to others' as an important personal value for yourself? For your parents?" When you have gone through the values, ask each student to list the values he or she crossed out. Invite discussion of these, if appropriate. Generate further discussion with questions like the following.

    ▶ How do your values differ from your family's values? How are they similar?

    ▶ Have differences in values caused conflict within your family?

    ▶ Do you expect that differences in values will cause conflict when you are an adult with a family of your own?

    ▶ Does there seem to be a "generation gap" in your family regarding values—between the adults and the children?

    ▶ If we assume that you are typical of your generation, can you identify any apparent trends regarding values?

3. Ask the students how their values fit in with their long-range career and lifestyle goals.

4. For closure, ask someone to summarize what has been discussed in the session. Encourage the students to consider their values when making their long-range plans for life.

a question of values

Name: _____

Under "Father," mark with an "X" the ten most significant values of your father/stepfather/male guardian.

Under "Mother," mark the ten most significant values of your mother/stepmother/female guardian.

Under "Self," mark the ten values you feel will be most significant to you as an adult.

Underline any values you have changed your mind about over the past few years.

Cross out any values that neither you nor your parents consider to be important.

	FATHER	MOTHER	SELF
marriage	_____	_____	_____
having children	_____	_____	_____
family closeness	_____	_____	_____
marital fidelity	_____	_____	_____
financial security	_____	_____	_____
health and fitness	_____	_____	_____
respect for the environment	_____	_____	_____
tolerance for others' differing lifestyles	_____	_____	_____
religious faith	_____	_____	_____
involvement in an organized church or temple	_____	_____	_____
loyalty to friends	_____	_____	_____
freedom from physical pain or discomfort	_____	_____	_____
meaningful work	_____	_____	_____
political activity	_____	_____	_____
high moral behavior	_____	_____	_____
community involvement	_____	_____	_____
service to others	_____	_____	_____
leisure activities	_____	_____	_____
material possessions	_____	_____	_____
a beautiful home and surroundings	_____	_____	_____
change, variety, and adventure	_____	_____	_____
travel	_____	_____	_____
creative self-expression	_____	_____	_____

a question of values continued

	FATHER	MOTHER	SELF
achievement	_____	_____	_____
being rational and reasonable	_____	_____	_____
self-understanding, introspection	_____	_____	_____
self-sacrifice	_____	_____	_____
self-discipline	_____	_____	_____
commitment to social justice for all people	_____	_____	_____
a high level of activity, busy-ness	_____	_____	_____
inner peace, peace of mind	_____	_____	_____
love and affection	_____	_____	_____
a good reputation	_____	_____	_____
personal freedom	_____	_____	_____
education	_____	_____	_____
family honor, family name, family history	_____	_____	_____

focus: the self
success and failure

The words "success" and "failure" are tossed around a lot at all age levels. But what do they mean? Does money make one successful? Does education? Does respect? Does lack of money, education, or respect mean failure? Who defines those words for us? Do people at various socioeconomic levels interpret success and failure differently?

Adolescents with high ability are not the only ones who feel intense pressure to succeed, although they may feel it especially keenly. Adolescents at all intellectual and socioeconomic levels wrestle with these terms and the feelings that are associated with them during their school years. This session gives them a chance to talk about their unique present and future expectations and anxieties regarding success and failure.

objectives

- Students learn that definitions of the words "success" and "failure" vary considerably among their peers.

- They consider that success and failure do not have to be connected to money and status.

- They think about the future and what might contribute to their feeling successful as adults.

suggestions

1. Introduce the topic with a reference to a person who is considered "successful." You may want to present an example from a current newspaper or magazine. Then ask the students to define the terms "success" and "failure," in that order. Their definitions and interpretations may vary considerably, and you can expect this activity to generate discussion. Encourage the students to express a wide variety of opinions.

   If your group includes students with high capability, you may want to tie in this discussion with the idea of perfectionism. (For a session on perfectionism, see pages 40–43.)

2. Focus on success, failure, and how they relate to school life. Invite the students to apply the terms to various aspects of school life—academic, extracurricular, social. Ask questions like the following.

107

▶ Can a student be successful and not be well-known in school?

▶ Can a person be successful but *feel* as if he or she is a failure?

▶ Does success depend on other people knowing about it? Does failure?

▶ What causes success to "go to someone's head"?

▶ When is "failure" especially devastating?

▶ When have you experienced "success"?

▶ When have you experienced "failure"?

▶ Has anyone ever used the term "failure" to describe something you have done?

▶ What has influenced your way of interpreting the words "success" and "failure"?

▶ Who has helped to define these terms for you?

▶ Who do you want to tell when you feel successful? Is that person someone who influences your direction and values?

▶ How much do you worry about failure?

▶ Is it important to "learn how to fail"? What good might that do?

▶ Do males and females view "success" and "failure" differently?

3. Shift the focus to adulthood with questions like the following.

▶ Do "success" and "failure" mean the same to adults as they do to teenagers?

▶ What will make you feel successful when you are 30? 40? 50? When you are retired?

▶ What might make you feel like a "failure" when you are an adult?

4. Encourage the students to think of success in general terms. Ask questions like the following.

▶ What are "successful" relationships?

▶ Is "success" having contributed to someone else's happiness?

▶ Is it having someone's respect?

▶ Is it knowing that you have done your best in life?

▶ Is it being able to appreciate life?

▶ Is it being able to put your natural talents and abilities to use?

▶ Is it contentment?

▶ Does our society have a too-narrow view of success?

5. For closure, ask one group member or a few to define the terms "success" and "failure" again. What did they hear during the discussion? Did any comments surprise them? Did they all agree?

focus: the self
being alone vs. being lonely

background

Some adolescents—and adults, too—are afraid to be alone. A solitary weekend evening is uncomfortable at best and anxiety-laden at worst. They might believe that the world is busily and happily out there having fun and they are left out, or that spending weekends alone is their lot for the rest of their life. On the other hand, some adolescents—and adults—love solitude and savor it as a time for renewal apart from the pressures and demands of life. Solitude can help people to be in touch with themselves.

Perhaps the differences in how people perceive being alone are related to predisposition toward introversion or extroversion. Introverts tend to find sustenance from within and appreciate time alone to recoup their energy, while extroverts tend to prefer people contact for sustenance and renewal. (For more on this topic, see the Recommended Resource.) Or perhaps it is more complex than that. For some in both groups, being alone can cause insecurity and fear. Maybe those feelings urge them into socializing or relationships.

Whether simple or complex, being alone vs. being lonely is an issue worth discussing, especially during the formative years. There is value in just talking about it.

recommended resource

Keirsey, D., and Bates, M. *Please Understand Me* (Del Mar, CA: Prometheus Nemesis Book Co., 1984). Information regarding introversion and extroversion, as well as other personality types.

objectives

- Students learn more about themselves by thinking about how comfortable they are being alone.
- They practice articulating their feelings about being alone vs. being lonely and discover similarities within the group.
- They explore some possible benefits of being alone.
- They consider ways to alleviate loneliness.

suggestions

1. Introduce the topic by asking the students to define the terms "alone" and "lonely."

2. Begin a discussion about being alone vs. being lonely by asking questions like the following.

   ▶ How easy is it for you to be alone? Is it scary?

   ▶ How uncomfortable are you walking down the halls in school alone? Going shopping by yourself?

   ▶ How do you feel about being at home alone on a weekend night? On a weekday night? Does one seem better or worse than the other?

   ▶ How do you feel about silence? Do you like it, or are you uneasy with it? Do you need to have music playing or the television on to fill up the silence?

   ▶ What seems to be your family "style" when it comes to quietness and being alone? Do your parents value solitude and quiet? How can you tell?

3. Turn the group's attention toward possible benefits of being alone. Ask questions like the following.

important

As always, there are no "right" or "wrong" responses to any of these questions. Simply let the students respond, encourage them to be honest about their feelings, and actively listen to what they say.

   ▶ Does "alone" always mean "lonely"?

   ▶ Can loneliness have a good purpose? Can it instruct?

   ▶ Can it inspire people to make positive changes in their lives?

   ▶ Is it possible to become too dependent on relationships, on socializing, on being around other people all the time?

   ▶ How can a person use time alone, now and then, for personal benefit?

4. If the group enjoys puzzling over "why" questions, ask them to consider reasons for their feelings about being alone vs. being lonely. If being alone causes feelings of insecurity and fear, what are the fears?

5. Encourage them to explore ways to alleviate loneliness and give themselves permission to be alone.

6. For closure, ask someone to summarize the session. Thank them for contributing to the discussion and wish them well as they strive to become more comfortable with themselves.

focus: the self
a personal symbol

- Students think about who they are and what they value.
- They communicate a personal symbol thoughtfully and sensitively.

important

At the session immediately preceding this one, instruct the students to bring something to the next session that "symbolizes" them. Explain that this might be something that represents who they are or what they value, or it might be something that "sums them up." The symbol cannot be a word, even though words are symbols. Rather, it must be something they can touch, hold, and show to the group. If it cannot actually be carried to the group, a photograph or drawing will suffice.

Clarify the assignment as needed, according to the students' level of abstract thinking. Tell them that you trust them to take the assignment seriously and give it some thought. Reassure them that when they present and tell about their symbol, they will be treated with sensitivity and respect. If they have trouble thinking of something to bring, invite them to see you individually for some help.

Although this activity is appropriate for any group, my experience has shown that it works best for groups that are fairly homogeneous in ability.

suggestions

1. Begin by asking the students to show the group their personal symbol and explain why it represents something about them. Remind the group to be courteous and respectful during this "show-and-tell," since it involves some degree of risk for everyone.

2. Ask, "Is there anyone who would have had a much different symbol a few years ago?" Allow time for discussion. Then ask, "Is there anyone who would have brought the same symbol to group a few years ago?" Again, allow time for discussion.

3. For closure, thank the students for sharing their symbols and for giving the assignment careful thought. If appropriate, tell them that you are sure that they all know each other better now.

focus
the self
and others

focus: the self and others

This section of *Talk with Teens about Self and Stress* is meant to help students explore themselves in relationship with others. It invites them to consider how they relate to those who are important in their world, including peers and significant adults, and how this affects their self-concept, behavior, choices, and decision making.

Adolescents wonder how they are seen by others their age. They are both critical and self-critical, and they may not have an accurate "read" on what kind of image they present socially.

From the adults in their world, they have received powerful messages. Perhaps because of these messages, they may have trouble relating to people in authority. They may find it difficult to ask for advice. If the adults in their world have not been reliable, adolescents may feel that if they "leaned" on someone they would find no support. In some cases, their families might look to *them* for crucial support, perhaps to a degree inappropriate for their age. Some students have great family responsibilities. They may be taking care of others' needs, but may not know how to ask to have their own needs met. Of course, some adolescents receive encouraging and supporting messages from adults, and they may be secure and well balanced as a result.

A discussion group gives students an opportunity to discover what they have in common with their peers. They are all negotiating a complex period in their lives. Honest, open dialogue and interaction can help them to feel less lonely, different, or "weird." There is comfort in knowing that others are going through similar struggles. Being supported—*in relationship*—can shed new light on their world and their place in it. Ultimately, it can lead to the development of confidence, patience, tolerance, and a more positive outlook on life.

general objectives

- Students consider how others affect their attitudes and behaviors.
- They learn more about how others perceive them.
- They gain comfort in knowing that others share their concerns.
- They examine how they deal with people in authority.
- They identify personal needs and consider strategies for getting them met.
- They recognize the need for tolerance and compassion.

focus: the self and others
how others see us

- Students acknowledge how they believe others see them.
- They learn how they are perceived by members of the group.
- They learn whether others' perceptions of them match their perceptions of themselves.
- They explore the importance of clothing style, facial expression, posture, walk, and other body language in communication and in image-making.

1. Have the students complete the "How Others See Me, How I See Myself" activity sheet (page 119).

2. Encourage them to share, in turn, what they wrote about themselves in Part I of the activity sheet. You might begin by modeling and sharing your own list.

3. Follow up by asking each student if any of the perceptions they listed make them feel uncomfortable, or if any might be inaccurate.

4. After each student has finished sharing, ask the group as a whole if they heard any discrepancies among the various perceptions. Encourage them to express any surprise or disbelief they may have felt about some perceptions—or their support for certain perceptions.

5. Discuss how nonverbal messages affect the way people perceive each other and themselves. Ask questions like the following.

    ▶ What kinds of nonverbal messages do people send?

    ▶ Are there any specific nonverbal messages which suggest that someone is arrogant? Nervous? Critical? Uptight? Happy? Content? Tired? Secure? Insecure? Confident about his or her appearance? Self-conscious? Sad? Depressed? Angry? Irritated? Frustrated?

117

6. Have the students look at what they wrote in Part II of the activity sheet. Invite volunteers to share what they wrote, focusing on one student at a time. A few minutes might be devoted to that one individual, with group members giving their various perceptions. Then ask that student if there is anything he or she would like to ask the others. (Examples: "Do I seem arrogant?" "Do you think of me as boring and uninteresting?" "Am I too talkative?" "Do you see me as a friendly person?" "Am I fun to be around?")

7. For closure, either summarize the experience yourself, perhaps by speaking of your feelings during the exercise, or ask one or more students to share their feelings. Group members might also summarize any personal discoveries or insights, particularly about nonverbal messages.

how others see me, how i see myself

Name: _____

PART I

Complete each sentence with at least three adjectives.

My mother thinks I am _____

_____

_____

My father thinks I am _____

_____

_____

My teachers think I am _____

_____

_____

My friends think I am _____

_____

_____

People who don't know me and who never have heard me talk, but just see me in the halls at school, probably think I am _____

_____

_____

People who know me usually appreciate my

_____

_____

_____

I think I am _____

_____

_____

PART II

List the names of all the people in this group. Leave some space after each person's name. Use the space to write down your first impression of him or her, no matter how long ago it was. If you can't recall your first impression, describe the person's current "image"—what that person communicates by the way he or she dresses, stands, walks, gestures; by style, facial expressions, etc.

_____

_____

_____

_____

_____

_____

_____

_____

_____

_____

_____

_____

_____

_____

_____

_____

_____

_____

focus: the self and others

encouragement and discouragement

It is relatively easy for someone who feels satisfied and secure in life to encourage others through good wishes, support, compliments, and other actions. (Of course, there is always the possibility that people are supportive of others in ways they wish *others* would be supportive of *them*.) In contrast, it can be difficult for someone who is highly competitive and critical of others to offer encouragement. If encouragement has not been role modeled at home, the instinct and skills needed to encourage others may not be present.

Sometimes it is equally difficult to *receive* support and encouragement. We may be concerned about appearing arrogant or self-absorbed if we accept compliments too readily. Or we may feel unworthy of compliments we receive because we think poorly of ourselves. Whatever the feeling involved, receiving compliments, like giving them, is a social skill, learned from models, that becomes smoother with practice. A group of supportive peers is a good place to practice.

objectives

- Students recognize encouragement and discouragement in their lives.
- They learn about the power of encouragement and discouragement from others, and about how the words and behaviors of others help to "define" us.
- They consider their own power and ability to encourage and discourage others.
- They practice some skills in, and gain awareness about, expressing support in the form of compliments.

suggestions

1. Introduce the topic. Invite the students to list on paper those people who encourage them and, in a separate column, those who discourage them.

2. Encourage the students to share their lists and tell how the various individuals encourage or discourage them. Afterward, you might ask them if they feel down or depressed in a particular person's presence, or defensive about who they are, or apologetic, or incompetent. Then

120

ask, "Who gives you unconditional support—affirmation with no strings attached, no conditions to meet, no 'tests' to pass?"

3. Introduce the idea of giving compliments as a way to encourage others. Ask questions like the following and allow for discussion after any or all as time permits.

   ▶ Are you used to getting and giving compliments in your family? Among your friends?

   ▶ Is it difficult for you to give compliments? To receive compliments? Which is more difficult?

   ▶ Does academic or social competition with others interfere with your giving and receiving compliments?

   ▶ Do you feel that you don't know how to give and receive compliments gracefully?

   ▶ Are there particular situations and times in your life when it's especially difficult to give or receive comments?

4. Ask experienced compliment-givers to demonstrate their skills, with the group giving feedback. Ask them also to demonstrate *receiving* compliments, with group feedback.

5. Acknowledge that it's normal to have mixed feelings about giving or receiving compliments. Present some examples that might include the following, and ask students for their perceptions and interpretations.

   ▶ We wonder if accepting a compliment will cost us something later. (Will "I love your new jacket" turn into "May I borrow your new jacket?" Do I owe friendship in return for a compliment? Do I have to remember to return the compliment tomorrow?)

   ▶ We feel as if we have measured up to the compliment-giver's standards, and we worry that we will have to keep meeting those standards. (Does "Good work!" mean "I expect you to keep getting/doing 100 percent"?)

   ▶ Some compliments seem routine and not heartfelt. How can we be sure?

   ▶ We worry that we are being manipulated. (Is "I like your sweater" meant to ensure your vote in the student council election? Is "You do such a good job of cleaning the bathroom" meant to get you to accept that dreaded chore *every* week at home? Does "You're so responsible" mean that you'll soon have to accept *more* responsibility?)

   ▶ We wonder if our reactions are being tested. (When someone says "Great haircut," are we supposed to smile and say "Thanks," or do and say nothing?)

Most of us probably accept compliments that fit our image of ourselves. Even then, we may feel torn between accepting the compliments gracefully and worrying about appearing arrogant.

Encourage the students to accept—and give—compliments when the moment is ripe, for such opportunities are quickly lost. Discourage them from automatically rejecting or deflecting compliments or being suspicious of compliment-givers.

6. For closure, have the students arrange themselves in pairs and exchange compliments, with the receiver simply saying "Thank you." They can then rearrange themselves into new pairs and repeat the exchange, ending the session on a positive note.

focus: the self and others
those who influence

background

This session can be particularly valuable for students at risk, since it gives them an opportunity to sort out the influences on their lives (both positive and negative) and to discover which ones provoke strong responses (both positive and negative). It is a good topic for all other students as well, including adolescents with high capability, who seem to deal intensely with others' expectations and influences as their "antennae" pick up stimuli from their various environments.

objectives

- Students enhance self-awareness through thinking and talking about those who have influenced their values and direction, both positively and negatively.

- Students at risk gain perspective on themselves through thinking about those who might have influenced them to respond to school, to other people, or to life in general in ways that are not productive or satisfying.

- Students gain experience in acknowledging others who have influenced them positively.

suggestions

1. Begin the session by asking the students to list on paper 5-10 people who have had a *positive* influence on their values and direction. Then ask them to list 5-10 people who have had a *negative* influence on their values and direction.

   If they want to, they might make a separate column of people who have influenced them *not* to be like them. If they need help understanding this concept, ask, "Is there anyone you have promised yourself *never* to be like?"

   Students' lists may include peers, family members, teachers, and other adults. Their lists may also include people they have read about in biographies or heard about on the news who have strongly influenced their values and direction.

2. Encourage the students to share their lists. Invite them to give a reason for listing each person.

3. Generate discussion by asking questions like the following.

   ▶ Does your list of positive "influencers" include mostly people who have influenced your values, or mostly people who have influenced your direction? What about your list of negative "influencers"?

   ▶ Do your lists include mostly family members or persons outside of your family? Males or females? People who are very similar to each other or many different types of people? Short-term acquaintances or long-term acquaintances? People you know personally or people you have read about or heard about? Rebels or conformists? Competitive achievers or laid-back types? Optimists or pessimists?

   ▶ Is there one key individual on your positive list who has influenced you more than anyone else? If so, what might that person wish for you? Does that person know how much you have been influenced by him or her? Are you in contact with that person?

4. Some adolescents may have had few or no positive "influencers" in their life. If you notice that any students in your group seem unable to list positive "influencers," encourage them to describe the kind of person they would listen to, believe, and be positively influenced by. They might also be willing to tell how the *absence* of positive "influencers" has affected them. If they become angry or sad while exploring this sensitive topic, support their feelings and encourage them to talk. Remind the group of the need for confidentiality.

   Sometime before the group experience ends, you might try to match these students with adults who were troubled or at risk as adolescents but have since grown up to be successful, contributing members of the community. Perhaps you can arrange some regular contact for a period of time so that the students can experience some outside-of-school, outside-of-family influence on their self-image, values, and direction.

5. For closure, ask the students to write a note of acknowledgment and thanks to one of the people on their list of positive "influencers." You may want to mention that a note to a parent or other close relative can be especially touching and appreciated; in many families, such messages are never communicated or are thought of too late. Tell the students that they may choose to send their notes or not. They may leave when they finish writing their notes.

focus: the self and others
uniquenesses and similarities

- Students learn more about how they are different from others and how they are similar.

- Those who feel that no one else is as "different" as they are will feel more connected to others their age, regardless of their level of involvement in school.

1. Introduce the topic briefly. Explain that today you will spend time exploring uniquenesses and similarities, and you will do it in an unusual way.

2. Have the students line up along one wall of the room (or form an angle along two sides). Tell the students that they have just formed a "continuum." Designate one end of the continuum as "to a great extent/a lot" and the other end as "not at all." Explain that you are going to read a series of statements. As you read each statement, the students should physically move to the point on the continuum that best represents where they feel they belong.

3. Read aloud each statement from "Uniquenesses and Similarities: A Continuum Activity" on page 126. After each statement, and after students have found their places on the continuum, select two or three students to explain why they placed themselves where they did. If time is short, do this only for selected statements. (NOTE: This is the kind of activity that needs to move along quickly, and it is best not to spend too long considering individual statements. Do not continue this activity into the next session.)

4. For closure, ask the students if they noticed any "trends" in their group. Are they a rather homogeneous group of creative, flexible, distractible, impulsive students, or are they more perfectionistic, organized, and orderly? Can anyone offer a general statement describing the group?

uniquenesses and similarities:

A CONTINUUM ACTIVITY

1. I like tough challenges and feel best when I am challenged.

2. I am cool in a crisis, and I can even lead others in a crisis.

3. I can change direction easily when I am doing something—for example, if suddenly someone wants/needs to do something different or do it in a new way.

4. I am organized in almost all aspects of my life.

5. I am a dreamer, spending a great deal of time in fantasies.

6. I work rapidly in whatever I do.

7. I am a highly creative person.

8. I am a perfectionist in almost everything I do.

9. I prefer to work alone, rather than with others, on most things.

10. I prefer to be alone, rather than with others, if I have a choice.

11. I am quick to respond to almost all situations.

12. I am impulsive, and I often wish I would have thought first before doing something.

13. I can work effectively without encouragement from someone else.

14. I like to work with my hands.

15. I am quite critical of others.

16. I worry a lot.

focus: the self and others
responding to authority

Many adolescents do not deal well with authority. When a teenager is involved in significant conflict with Dad or Mom, that conflict may carry over into school in the form of resistance to an authority figure of the same gender. Parental rigidity regarding child-rearing and/or harsh discipline can also lead to frustration and acting out on the part of the adolescent.

When one parent is absent, anger over that situation might spill over into conflict with the caretaking parent and also might affect relationships with adults in school. If there is no male authority figure in the family, male adolescents sometimes communicate, "I basically raised myself. Don't anybody tell *me* what to do!" They may respond to "orders" from male teachers, bosses, administrators, coaches, or police officers with automatic and intense resistance. Or they may target female teachers or other authority figures. Male students whose fathers have dominated their mothers sometimes expect to do the same with female teachers. Female adolescents may have similar problems dealing with authority, depending on their family situation.

If parental discipline is arbitrary and capricious, a child might be quick to indict "the system" when it seems inconsistent, when it "plays favorites," or when teachers and tests seem unfair. All of these responses can have a disastrous effect on academic achievement and comfort at school.

Children are fundamentally complex and resilient. There are many adolescents whose family situations do not lead to school problems, and there are countless well-balanced individuals from well-functioning families. Of course, a lack of obvious problems does not necessarily mean that a student feels no anger or rage. The student may have decided that such feelings will not interfere with his or her relationships, or both the student and the family may simply be unaccustomed to expressing feelings. Sometimes the response to having just one parent at home is to develop a relationship with a teacher, coach, or boss who is the same gender as the absent parent. Sometimes a child whose parenting has been inadequate or inconsistent looks to the school for nurturance.

A student may resist authority for reasons other than parental absence or abuse. For example, sometimes one or both parents are broadly "anti-system" and have long role modeled resistance to authority. A child might

127

be loyal to a family tradition of troublemaking. Or perhaps there is a large reservoir of rage over parents who are too controlling, too full of expectations, or too caught up in the child's life. As with all of these situations, such a child may come from any socioeconomic level.

Whatever the reasons, or seeming lack of reasons, difficulty with authority can continue to be a lifelong problem. Employment may eventually be affected, as can marriage and the next generation of parent-child relationships.

There is another side of the authority issue that may have affected those who seem to be fitting in well at school. Compliant students, and high achievers, too, can have problems with authority in the sense that they *always* defer to it. Perhaps they never question authority, they always do what they are told, they might not think for themselves, and they might not be able to respond creatively to life situations that demand a flexible response. They may be afraid to question anything or anyone, whether it be a demagogue, a cult leader, a corrupt boss, or an abusive spouse. They might *want* to be told what to do in any complex situation.

There is also the possibility that an adolescent's cultural background does not encourage challenging authority or does not promote individualistic thinking either at home or at school. Such cultural attitudes may cause conflict with peers or teachers in the dominant culture.

A discussion group can give adolescents a chance to explore their responses to authority in a supportive, rational, safe environment, with an adult whose main function is to listen. "Just talking" can help them better understand themselves as they relate to others.

objectives

- Students discover that there are many ways to respond to authority and many possible reasons for that variety of responses.

- They learn that unquestioning compliance with authority might be as problematic as automatic resistance.

- They consider why they respond to authority as they do, and, if there are problems, whether they might consider making some changes.

suggestions

1. Introduce the topic and have the students complete the "Responding to Authority" two-page activity sheet (pages 130–131), which gives them a chance to think about several authority figures in their lives.

   The activity sheet performs a "sorting" function that elicits more specific comments than oral discussion alone. Writing down specific examples helps students to be objective and to see possible patterns. This is not to say that discussion of student's *feelings* about authority should be avoided during this session. It is also important to assess repetition and habits, and writing can assist in that process.

2. Encourage the students to share their written responses and/or comment on the patterns they see. Ask questions like the following to generate discussion.

   ▶ Does your list of authority figures include all males? All females? Some of each?

   ▶ Are there differences between how you respond to females in authority and how you respond to males in authority?

   ▶ When you have problems with authority, are they mostly at school? Or are they also at home and at work?

   ▶ Are your problems at school mostly with your classroom teachers, or are they also with adults who coach and advise extracurricular activities?

   ▶ Do you have problems with one parent more than the other? If so, are your problems at school mostly with persons of the same gender and/or personality as that parent?

   ▶ What price do you pay for resisting authority?

   ▶ Have you made any changes recently in dealing with authority? If so, are you feeling less stress in this area of your life?

   ▶ If you have few or no apparent problems with authority, why do think that is the case? Is it because of cultural attitudes? Have you had few negative experiences with parental authority? Have certain experiences made you hesitant to question authority figures?

3. Time permitting, selectively and sensitively communicate some of the thoughts in the background information. (NOTE: This is entirely optional, since there is sufficient value in just talking about this issue.)

4. For closure, invite summary statements from one or more students. Did they gain any insights from this session? Was it helpful to hear from others in the group about dealing with authority?

responding to authority

Name: _____

1. List the adult authority figures in your life—people who give you advice, suggestions, or orders. Describe their position (teacher, coach, father, mother, etc.). Then tell how you typically respond to their authority.

NAME	POSITION	YOUR TYPICAL RESPONSE
a.		
b.		
c.		
d.		
e.		

2. If you have problems with the authority of any of the people listed above, what usually "sets you off"?

_____

_____

3. Does it appear that you have trouble with only certain *types* of authority figures? If so, explain.

_____

_____

4. Do you feel the need to "fight the system" in every part of your life?

_____

_____

5. Do you have any "unfinished business" with people whose authority you have trouble accepting? (For example, are you angry about something they did?) If you do not, go on to question #6. If you do, complete this question.

List any people who fit this category:

_____

_____

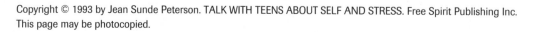

responding to authority continued

What feelings surface when you are confronted by any of these people?

_____

_____

What feelings do you have *after* a confrontation?

_____

_____

What are your options for responding to these people?

_____

_____

Can you think of anything that would change your response to their authority?

_____

_____

6. If you have no obvious problems with anyone you listed in #1, why do you think you respond fairly positively to their authority?

_____

_____

_____

7. Do you think your parents have treated you fairly?

_____

_____

_____

8. If you do not deal well with authority in general, what sacrifices are you making by having that conflict in your life?

_____

_____

_____

focus: the self and others
giving ourselves away

objectives

- Students consider what it means to be a "giving" person.
- They think about how they do or do not fit that description.
- They ponder the positive and negative consequences of being a "giver."

suggestions

1. Ask the students if they can think of people who seem to be "givers" in life. Explain that these might be individuals who are always "giving" of themselves—to their boyfriend or girlfriend, spouse, family, friends, or community.

   Ask, "What do you think it means to be a 'giver'?" Expect that for most students this will have only positive connotations, since the idea of "giving" and of being a "giver" is rarely discussed in negative terms.

2. Have the students consider the positives of being a "giver." They might mention the satisfaction of doing good deeds, the benefits to those who receive whatever the "giver" is giving, the fact that a "giver" is usually seen as generous rather than selfish, and so on.

3. Ask the group, "Is it possible to give too much?" Reassure them that you are not questioning the motives and value of volunteering, or the inspiring, selfless actions that enhance our lives and inspire others. Instead, explain that you are asking them to think about *excessive* giving and selflessness. Ask, "Can you think of any reason to be concerned about giving too much?"

4. Generate discussion by asking questions like the following, or let the students determine the direction with their own questions or suggestions. In deciding which questions to ask, be sensitive to your students' developmental level.

   ◗ How do we learn to give? (Examples: role models, encouragement, rewards.)

   ◗ How might being a giver help to meet someone's own needs?

   ◗ Can giving send messages about what the giver wants for himself or herself?

- What else might motivate a person to a high level of giving? (Examples: the need to "give back what has been given," to make life meaningful, to make order out of chaos, to overcome shame, to "fix what is broken" in oneself by helping others, to fill up personal emptiness, and so on.)

- Can a giver neglect himself or herself in the process of excessive giving to others? In what ways? (Examples: poor health, no time for leisure or relaxation, not taking care of oneself.)

- If a giver directs all of his or her attention outside the home, what might be neglected? (Examples: family relationships, responsibilities at home.)

- What might it be like to be in a relationship with an excessive giver?

- What might it be like to be the child of an excessive giver?

- Do children sometimes feel that they have to take on adult levels of responsibility at home? Even though this may teach valuable skills and help a family to survive, consider how it might affect the child. (Examples: the need to grow up too soon, the feeling that hard work and responsibility are the only things that matter, the belief that selflessness is the only route to satisfaction and fulfillment.)

5. Be aware that some students in your group may well be excessive givers. Ask the group what advice they would give to someone who fits this category. Encourage the givers in your group to think about other ways to feel valued. Guide the discussion toward the idea of paying healthy attention to one's own needs. Ask, "How much 'selfishness' is the right amount? How can you tell?"

6. For closure, ask for volunteers to share their personal insights into today's session and the insights gained from the discussion.

focus: the self and others
best advice

When we are growing up, it seems that adults are always giving us advice. Whether we pay attention at the time or ignore everything they say, we may surprise ourselves later by remembering—and even following—some of the advice we receive. Sometimes we do not even know we are following it. Sometimes we make sure we don't follow it.

Advice may recommend a course of action, warn against danger, or cause us to re-examine certain behaviors. When we respect the person who is giving the advice, we listen and may act on what we hear, knowing that the advice might make a difference in our lives.

This session gives students a chance to chuckle over often-repeated admonitions or warnings they heard as children or have heard as adolescents, and to reflect on powerful messages that have had a lasting effect on them.

objectives

- Students reflect on various bits of advice given to them by the adults in their lives.
- They consider how the advice has affected their direction, behavior, and attitudes.

suggestions

1. Begin by asking the group to brainstorm some areas in which people generally receive advice as they are growing up. Responses might include the following.

food	health
safety	strangers
hitchhikers	driving
sex	dating
women	men
alcohol and other drugs	career choice
cleanliness	chores
clothing	personal appearance

134

2. Have the students list on paper some specific bits of advice they have received in 4-5 of these areas, or consider one area at a time orally.

3. Ask, "How have you followed the advice you have been given? How has it affected your direction, behavior, and attitudes?"

4. Ask, "What is the *worst* piece of advice you have ever been given?" Allow time for discussion. Then ask, "What is the *best* piece of advice you have ever been given? What made it so valuable to you?" Again, allow time for discussion.

5. Invite the group to remember and share examples of advice given to them when they were very young. They may find humor in some of these simplistic warnings, especially about safety. They might also find humor in warnings they have received about sex and relationships.

6. For closure, remind the students that it is good to think about the things that affect our direction, behavior, and attitudes. You might ask for a volunteer to summarize what was discussed, or invite the students to comment on the most interesting or most thought-provoking advice they heard in group today.

focus: the self and others
who can we lean on?

Everyone needs help now and then. There are times when we all need advice, instruction, encouragement, or simply someone to listen. When adults need help, they call on the plumber, the mechanic, the carpenter, the physician, the financial adviser, the therapist, or the minister. When adolescents need help—for academic assistance, counseling, instruction in a skill, or advice in life—they may not know who to ask, or they may be reluctant or unwilling to ask. They are probably more likely to ask a peer than an adult. Even then, they may feel threatened by the mere fact of needing something.

For students of high ability, it can be especially difficult to "lean on" someone. They may have heard—and taken to heart—the directive "If you're so smart, figure it out yourself." They, and others as well, may believe that asking for help is "weak" or threatens their image of competence. As a result, they may suffer alone when they are hurting emotionally. They may find it hard to ask a teacher or professor for academic help. They do not seem to understand that it is normal and very human to need help—both in areas of strength and in areas of relative weakness.

Students at risk may also find it very difficult to ask for help. Like many their age, they may have put up barriers between themselves and significant adults in their lives. They may feel that no one could possibly understand their situation well enough to help. They may also have trouble showing "weakness."

This session invites students to explore the idea of asking for help when and where help is needed. It can be beneficial for adolescents to hear others speak honestly about confused feelings in this regard. A caring adult and a supportive group of peers can "give permission" to ask for help.

objectives

- Students learn that it is normal, human, and healthy to need assistance.
- They explore their feelings in regard to asking for help in various areas.

1. Introduce the topic by asking the students to think of the last time they asked someone for help—at school, at home, with friends, or on the job. Encourage them to share these situations with the group. Be willing to start the discussion by sharing an example from your own life.

2. Ask, "Are there times when it's hard to ask for help?" If students do not mention the following times and circumstances when help might be needed, introduce them into the discussion: for academic problems or direction; for advice about life; for problem-solving; for personal dilemmas; for social situations; for family problems. Explore with the group why it is difficult to ask for help in each situation. Does asking for help conflict with their self-image? Does it make them feel bad? Weak? Stupid?

3. Ask, "Are there certain people you would never ask for help? What about your father? Your mother? Siblings? Teachers? Certain teachers? Counselors? Certain counselors?" Encourage them to give reasons for their answers.

   If several students voice reluctance to talk to counselors, consider continuing this topic into another session. Invite a well-liked counselor to come in and speak with the group. Let the students ask questions about how counselors view their work, how they handle students with personal problems, what kinds of training counselors have, and what ethical principles guide them and other mental health professionals. Even if there are no apparent concerns about counselors, you might nevertheless invite someone in to address these areas, since probably only a few students in any school system are aware of them.

4. Remind them that the adult world revolves around help sought and received (see the background information), and that asking for help is *normal.* Acknowledge that many adults do not know how to ask for help, especially about emotional issues.

5. For closure, ask for volunteers to come up with a statement of advice about asking for help that would speak to students their age. Remind the group that people need to support each other in many ways. Remind them, too, that everyone needs help of various kinds throughout life, and that asking for help is a compliment to the person who is asked (even if he or she does not always see it that way).

focus: the self and others
gifts we would like from people who matter

background

Probably most people feel a "gap" somewhere in their lives. Children may long for time and attention from busy parents. Perhaps they yearn for a sign of appreciation or encouragement—or the absence of criticism, nagging, alcohol, television, or arguing. They may wish for support or kind words from brothers and sisters. Sometimes these wishes are easy to articulate, and sometimes they are not. This session can become a "wish list," honestly spoken and sympathetically received by a supportive group, willing to listen.

objectives

- Students focus on their needs and wants.
- They learn to express their feelings about significant people in their lives and what they most need from them.

suggestions

1. Introduce the topic in concrete terms by asking the group to tell about the best gifts/presents they ever received from someone who meant a lot to them. Encourage them to give more than one example.

2. Move into the abstract by asking the students to think of meaningful things they have been given by significant people in their lives that cannot be held, touched, or seen. Mention the following ideas if the students do not introduce them into the discussion.

attention	direction
love	unconditional love
friendship	concern
support	self-confidence
affection	encouragement
understanding	acceptance
role modeling	a shoulder to cry on
the right words at	instruction in a skill
a difficult time	or talent
a sense of fun	a place to relax
an appreciation for something	

3. Hand out the "My Wish List" activity sheet (page 140). Ask the group to think about what they wish they could get/have from various family members. Role model by mentioning something specific you wish each of your parents would give (or had given) to you.

4. Give the students a few moments to complete their activity sheets. Afterward, encourage the students to share their "wish lists."

5. For closure, you might summarize what you heard from the students and what wishes they seem to have in common. Or ask a volunteer to summarize the session.

my wish list

Name: _____

Write what you would most like to get or have from each family member. Remember, this should not be something you can hold, touch, or see.

From my mother: _____

From my father: _____

From my sister: _____

From my brother: _____

From _____ : _____

From _____ : _____

From _____ : _____

From _____ : _____

If you need ideas:

time	attention
unconditional support	affirmation
less competitiveness	less jealousy
less pressure	more concern
encouragement	honesty
less criticism	less tension
a hug	understanding
patience	advice
instruction in something	information
a compliment	better behavior

focus: the self and others
getting our needs met

Many people do not know how to ask for what they need. There may be many reasons why they find this difficult or impossible to do. Perhaps they prefer to do things for others—to be "givers" rather than "receivers." They might not want to be in debt to anyone. They might not want to give anyone the satisfaction of helping them. Perhaps poor self-esteem makes them feel unworthy of assistance. Maybe they are afraid of appearing weak. Maybe they do for others what they wish others would do for them. Whatever the explanation, their needs may go unmet, and they might feel sad, frustrated, and discouraged—perhaps without even knowing why.

Ideally, students should express their needs to teachers, and vice versa. If a student cannot learn by just hearing information, and if the teacher never uses visual aids, the student should say "It's hard for me to understand things when I can't see them, and I need a summary sheet to look at while you explain things." If a teacher cannot concentrate because of something a student is doing, the teacher should say "I have a hard time concentrating when you do that, and I need to concentrate to teach the class."

Ideally, people in relationships should express their needs. Boyfriends and girlfriends, husbands and wives, friends and lovers need to be able to say "I would like to be more involved in our decisions. Sometimes I feel left out," or "I would like you to be more involved in deciding what we do because I feel I'm in charge of that too much," or "I need to have you tell me how you feel about things. I need to have you say it in words," or "I wish we would plan more fun things to do," or "I need to be in touch with you more often," or "I need to get to places on time." Couples need to express their wishes and concerns about sex, yet many do not know how.

Ideally, parents should express their needs to their children: "I want you to come to the table when I call, because when you dawdle, I feel that you don't appreciate my work getting the meal ready," or "I need to know how long you will be using the car, since I might need to run an errand." And children should express their needs to their parents: "I feel invaded when you go through my papers in my room without my permission. I need to feel that my personal space is mine—private," or "I need to start making more of my own decisions. When you make decisions for me, I feel frustrated and dependent."

Relationships at home, at work, and with friends are enhanced when people are able to express their needs clearly and directly. This session will emphasize that reality and help students consider ways to express their personal needs.

objectives

- Students become more aware of the value of expressing personal needs clearly and directly.
- They clarify their own needs.
- They practice asking for what they need.

suggestions

1. Begin by conveying some of the general ideas in the background information. Then ask, "On a scale of 1 to 10, with 1 being 'very poorly' and 10 being 'very well,' how well do you express your needs to other people? Think of your parents, siblings, teachers, friends, employers, or boyfriend/girlfriend."

2. Hand out the "My Needs" activity sheet (page 144). Tell the group to read down the list quickly and put a check mark by any item that seems true for them.

3. Encourage the students to share their lists. Model by sharing yours first. Reassure the students that they need to mention only the items they feel comfortable sharing, and remind the group of the need for confidentiality.

4. Instruct the students to look back at the items they checked on their lists, circle anything they think they could *ask for*, and underline anything they think they could *do something about*, starting today.

5. When students seem ready to continue, invite each student to choose one item they circled and put it in the form of a request, as "practice." Explain that they should begin their request with "I." Encourage them to be clear, direct, and honest, and to phrase their request in a way that does not attack or demand. If a student has difficulty composing a request, ask if he or she would like to ask the group for help. If help is requested, the group can give suggestions.

   Then invite the students to share one or two items they underlined. Ask them to explain what they could do to meet those needs.

6. Begin a discussion about the difficulty most people have in addressing needs directly. Ask questions like the following.

   ‣ Do you ever drop hints about your needs or let your "moods" communicate them, and then feel angry or sad if no one "gets the message"?

   ‣ Do you sometimes use bad behavior to get the attention you need?

   ‣ Is your school performance connected in any way to your attempts to get your needs met?

> Do you ever do things for other people in the hope that they will do things for you?

> Do you think that asking for something you need is "wrong" or "not nice" or "too pushy"?

Invite comments on these and other indirect ways we try to communicate our needs.

7. Ask, "Is there anyone you know who does a good job of expressing his or her needs? What could you learn from him or her?"

8. Invite the students to imagine themselves as adults—as employees, spouses, parents. Ask, "How could learning how to ask for what you need benefit you in the future?"

9. For closure, ask one or more volunteers to summarize the session. What did they learn about themselves? About others? About asking for what they need? What did it feel like to express their needs?

my needs

Name: _____

Check anything from this list that you feel you need. If something you need is not on this list, add it to the end and check it, too.

____ someone to say, "I care about you"

____ attention

____ support in a personal dilemma

____ a hug

____ kind words

____ space

____ privacy at home

____ peace and quiet

____ less (or no) criticism from others

____ more contact with people

____ order

____ direction

____ kind words from my mom

____ kind words from my dad

____ a better relationship with a step-parent

____ peace with a sibling (or siblings)

____ a good night's sleep

____ a decent meal

____ a feeling of success

____ less stress

____ fewer demands on my time/more time to myself

____ fewer "pieces" in my complicated life

____ less chaos around me

____ less arguing with someone else

____ less arguing at home by others

____ a feeling of hope that things will improve

____ someone to listen

____ a conversation that doesn't get interrupted

____ someone to love

____ someone to love me

____ something to keep me busy

____ something to relieve boredom

____ teachers who care about me

____ a different teaching style in a teacher

____ teachers who can appreciate that I am going through a bad time right now

____ approval

____ respect from my peers

____ to lead

____ to be led

____ _____

____ _____

focus: the self and others
tolerance and compassion

In our increasingly pluralistic nation, tolerance and compassion are critical for smooth and mutually satisfying relationships among people who are different from each other. These qualities are probably vital to our national survival. How can we encourage them in young people so that they will not join the growing trend of gay-bashing, racial bigotry, hate groups, and narrow rigidity about who deserves fair and respectful treatment? Discussion groups offer at least a brief opportunity to raise awareness about these issues and to talk about the importance of promoting inter-personal and intercultural sensitivity.

This session is not meant to be anything more than a very basic treatment of personal and cultural values, multicultural issues, and human relations. All deserve in-depth study, and that is the realm of social studies. However, within the context of a trusting, caring group, it is appropriate to pose questions that provoke examination of some important feelings related to living in a complex, constantly changing world.

objectives

- Students consider the importance of tolerance and compassion in human relations.

- They also consider ways to develop these qualities in themselves and others.

important

Part of this session involves a discussion of hate groups. You should be prepared to present basic information about such groups—what they believe, what motivates them, who belongs to them, and so on. If possible, you may want to bring to the session some current or recent articles about hate groups from newspapers and magazines.

suggestions

1. Ask the students to define the terms "tolerance" and "compassion." If necessary, offer brief definitions. Examples for tolerance: "live and let live," "respecting individual differences," "not trying to change or hurt someone whose ideas and lifestyle are not the same as mine, even if I don't personally approve." Examples for compassion: "empathy," "understanding," "trying to understand without judging."

2. Invite the students to give examples of tolerance and compassion from the "real world"—things they have seen or experienced at school, in their family, at work, or in the community. If they cannot think of examples they have personally seen or experienced, they can tell of something they have heard or read about.

3. Generate discussion about tolerance by asking questions like the following.

   ▶ Does there seem to be a lot of tolerance in the world today, or only some? A little? None?

   ▶ Do you hear people speaking out *against* tolerance? What are some of the reasons they give for the need to be less tolerant?

   ▶ Do you see our society as becoming more tolerant or less tolerant? Give reasons or examples.

   ▶ Do you have any fears or anxieties about how various cultures in our country, or in the world, are getting along lately?

4. Turn the discussion to the topic of hate groups. Begin by presenting some of the information you prepared ahead of time. You might mention economic factors, fears, hate, anger, abuse, demagoguery, vulnerable minority populations, power differences among groups, misinformation, and religious and political trends. Then ask questions like the following.

   ▶ Have you ever seen or read anything about hate groups?

   ▶ Why do you think adolescents are attracted to hate groups?

   ▶ What makes young people especially vulnerable to their message?

   ▶ What *is* their message?

   ▶ What factors in society today seem to make people more willing to listen to such groups?

   ▶ What ethnic or cultural groups are currently being targeted by hate groups?

   ▶ What makes an ethnic or cultural group vulnerable to violence in a society?

   ▶ What are some common stereotypes of targeted groups?

5. Invite group members to explore and describe their own feelings regarding tolerance and compassion. Ask questions like the following.

  ▶ How tolerant and compassionate are you?

  ▶ How tolerant and compassionate is your family?

  ▶ Have you had contact during your life with people of other racial and cultural groups besides your own? If so, how much? What kind? How has that contact affected your ability to avoid stereotyping? To interact comfortably with people who are different from you?

  ▶ If an African-American couple (or Asian-American, Mexican-American, Native American, White, Russian, Guatemalan, Palestinian, etc.) moved next door to you, how would you feel?

  ▶ If a Jewish family (or Mormon, Jehovah's Witness, Pentecostal, Catholic, Presbyterian, Southern Baptist, etc.) moved next door to you, how would you feel?

  ▶ If a gay or lesbian couple moved next door to you, how would you feel?

  ▶ If you fell in love with someone from one of these groups, how would you or your family react?

  ▶ If one of your siblings planned to marry someone from one of these groups, how would you or your family react?

  ▶ If you would feel uncomfortable with a neighbor whose ethnic or religious background or sexual orientation was different from yours, what might cause you to feel that way? If you made your feelings clear, how do you think your neighbor might feel or respond?

  ▶ Have you been in a situation where you were in the minority? If so, how did you feel?

  ▶ If a hate group targeted your religion or culture, what would you do?

  ▶ Do you think it would be possible for your religion or culture to become the target of a hate group? Why or why not?

  ▶ Do you think you are personally vulnerable to the message of hate groups?

  ▶ What would you say to a member of a hate group who told you that "all immigrants should leave this country because they are taking jobs away from real Americans, bleeding the welfare system, and corrupting American values"?

  ▶ What are the potential strengths of a nation made up of many cultures?

  ▶ Why are tolerance and compassion important to our lives—to your life—today?

6. Ask the students to think about how we can develop tolerance and compassion in ourselves and in our children. Mention the following if they do not come up in the discussion: education, role modeling, making a conscious effort to learn about and get to know people whose backgrounds and beliefs may be different from ours.

7. For closure, ask if any group members would like to express their feelings of the moment about tolerance and compassion. Encourage them to continue educating themselves about the important issues mentioned during this session.

focus

stress

focus: stress

Mention the word "stress" to an adolescent, and you will have begun a serious conversation. Starting at an early age, most young people become well acquainted with the high stress of living in this culture. Parents bring home the stress of the workplace, or they suffer job loss, both of which have a ripple effect on the family. Because ours is a mobile society, there are moves and dislocations that cause stress. There are pressures at school, with some children coping well—and some not so well—with the demands of the system and the challenges of the social world. There may be illness, accidents, or other dramatic events that cause physical and emotional repercussions for months or years. For gifted students, their multipotentiality may cause stress. There are simply too many possible directions from which they may choose.

Stress is part of life—from growing up to growing old, facing change, facing illness, working, and caring for family members. Pessimism, trying to respond to everyone's needs, multiple responsibilities, and isolation all can heighten stress levels.

Consciously or unconsciously, families teach children coping skills. Some learn healthy and effective ways to cope with life's stressors. They talk about the stress they are experiencing, step back and gain perspective on stressful situations, and apply problem-solving techniques. They release tension through a healthy level of exercise, socializing, relaxation, diversion, or a deliberate change of pace and pattern. Others learn less healthy ways to cope with stress. They try to escape or deny it through alcohol and other drugs, overeating, workaholism, moving to a new location (the "geographic cure"), sleeping, daydreaming, or watching too much television. Some resort to tantrums or violence in the form of abuse. Others "cope" by blaming, scapegoating, punishing, or accepting a "victim" posture.

The sessions in this section of *Talk with Teens about Self and Stress* give students a chance to think about their stressors and to begin sorting them into two basic categories: what they can do something about, and what cannot be changed. Within the safe, supportive environment of the group, they can discuss their coping styles and perhaps begin to address their stressful situations more effectively.

Simply having a chance to talk about stress can be valuable. Your primary responsibility as group leader is to listen carefully to your students, hear what they are saying, indicate by your response that you have heard them, and commend them for their honesty and willingness to articulate complex issues and feelings.

general objectives

- Students learn more about stress.
- They learn to talk about stress, stressors, and stressful situations.
- They consider various ways to cope with stress.

focus: stress
what is stress?

objectives

- Students increase their understanding of stress.
- They discover similarities within the group regarding stress and stressors.
- They find out that people respond differently to similar stressors, depending on their personal makeup and how they interpret various situations.

important

All of the sessions in this section depend on group members having some understanding of stress and stressors. Be sure to present this session before proceeding to any of the other nine sessions on stress.

suggestions

1. Introduce the topic by asking the students to define the term "stress." If necessary, provide a few synonyms: anxiety, pressure, tension, worry, apprehension, burden. Then ask volunteers to tell what they know about stress. Afterward, introduce information from the following that was not brought up in the group discussion.

   ▶ Stress can be good. It can lead to high productivity, a good level of competitiveness, great performances, and high alertness. Some people even seek out stress, loving the adrenalin rush and performing better when the pressure is on.

   ▶ Excessive stress can cause problems if it is not coped with effectively. It can affect concentration, sleep, safety, and appetite. It can cause irritability, over-reactions to normal problems, self-blame, tearfulness, anxiety, depression, and panic attacks.

   ▶ Physical responses to stress include accelerated heartbeat (as the body prepares for fight or flight), cold extremities (as the capillaries constrict to make more blood available at the center of the body to protect the major organs), tight muscles, tense shoulders, a "pressure" headache, dry mouth, clammy hands, and/or stomach or intestinal distress.

> Prolonged periods of stress can lead to significant physical problems. Medical professionals see many physical maladies that may have their origins in stress. They also see patients with pain and distress but no apparent physical problems, and often conclude that the symptoms are related to stress.

> Most people seem to be vulnerable to excessive stress in a particular way. They may develop colds, diarrhea, stomach aches, headaches, skin problems, tense neck and shoulders, etc.

> Stress can result from having to do "something different"—for example, move to a new home, change schools, adjust to a new baby, start a new work assignment, start new kinds of school assignments, adjust to a loss.

2. Encourage the students to describe their own physical and emotional responses to stress. Ask, "What tells you that you are under stress? How do you behave? How do you feel? How does your body react?"

3. Ask the students to tell about stressful situations in their lives. Every so often, as a way of supporting those who are sharing, ask the group, "Does this sound familiar? Has anyone else experienced this?"

4. If appropriate for your group, ask questions like the following.

> Do you feel stress from competition (academic, athletic, arts, etc.)?

> Do you feel as if you are ahead intellectually but behind socially?

> Do you feel great pressure to achieve? From others? From yourself?

> Do you work slowly?

> Is needing/trying to please everyone a problem for you?

Consider inviting an expert to speak with your group as a follow-up session. This might be someone from a stress clinic, or an expert on biofeedback, meditation/relaxation, or yoga.

5. Ask the students if there is a specific stressor they need help coping with. Find out if the group has any suggestions.

6. For closure, invite volunteers to summarize what they have learned, felt, or thought about during this session.

focus: stress
sorting out the sources of stress

- Students learn that it can feel good to talk about stressors in their lives and feelings associated with them.

- They hear about the stressors of other group members, which helps to put theirs into perspective and also helps them to feel less alone in dealing with their stress.

- They evaluate various stressors and determine which ones are short-term and which are long-term, which can be remedied and which cannot.

- They learn that focusing on the present, as opposed to always looking anxiously to the future, can alleviate some stress.

- They explore whether making adjustments in their lives might enable them to concentrate on themselves in healthy ways and relieve some stress.

1. Introduce the topic with references to the session on stress and stressors, "What Is Stress?" on pages 153–154. Be sure to complete that session before proceeding to any of the others in this section. Share any other relevant information you have learned about stress and stressors, perhaps from recent newspaper or magazine articles.

2. Hand out the "Stress Boxes" activity sheet (page 158). Instruct the students to write the word "ME" in each of the small boxes along the bottom and connect the upper boxes to the lower boxes with straight lines. Then tell them to write the name or description of a *specific* stressor in each of the large boxes along the top. (Examples: "school" is not specific; "third period math class" is. "Family" is not specific; "my little sister invading my privacy" is. "Noise" is not specific; "the sound of airplanes flying over our house all night long" is.)

   When they have finished, ask them to darken and widen each connecting line according to how much stress they associate with that particular stressor. (The more stress, the darker and wider the line.) Then instruct them to write an "X" above each box containing a *short-term* stressor, a " + " above each box containing a stressor they could do

155

something about if they chose to, and a larger square around each box containing a *long-term* stressor that might be with them for many years—possibly for a lifetime.

important

During this activity, be alert for students who seem unable to discriminate among their stressors, or who have drawn dark, wide lines to all of them, which may indicate imminent overload. Arrange to meet with those students privately at some other time. You might invite them to talk to you about the stress they are experiencing. Or, depending on your assessment of the situation, you might suggest that they talk to a school counselor.

3. Encourage the students to share their stress boxes with the group. One way to do this is to list their stressors in order of intensity, and then explain which ones are short-term, which ones they could do something about if they chose to, and which ones (if any) might be long-term.

4. As group members share their stress boxes, encourage them or others to offer suggestions for coping and problem-solving. Following are some examples of stressors and suggestions.

   ▶ Short-term stressor: Too much make-up homework. Suggestions: Try harder to complete assignments on time; get better organized (use a calendar?) so you won't forget assignments.

   ▶ Short-term stressor: Can't find anything in my room. Suggestion: Clean the room so it's easier to find things.

   ▶ Short-term stressor: A big research paper that's due soon. Suggestions: Stop procrastinating and start working on it today. Break it down into smaller steps and finish one at a time.

   ▶ Short-term stressor: College applications. Suggestions: Try to get them done this weekend. Ask school counselor for help. Ask teachers for recommendations.

   ▶ Long-term stressor: A co-worker who doesn't do his or her share. Suggestions: Be more assertive. Set limits. Talk to him or her directly.

   ▶ Long-term stressor: No privacy at home. Suggestions: Set limits. Put a lock on the bedroom door. Hide the diary.

   ▶ Long-term stressor: Constant family fights. Suggestions: Set up a family meeting to discuss alternatives. See if the family will agree to a "count-to-10-before-you-yell" rule. Break the pattern by not responding in the usual way.

   ▶ Long-term stressor: Worries about college. Suggestions: Talk to a school counselor. Talk to someone who graduated from college recently. Talk to someone who currently attends college.

To conclude this part of the discussion, you might say something like this: "We can't eliminate all stressors from our lives, but we can learn to accept their presence, and we can alter the way we *respond* to them. We can also make sure that we take care of our health, so that during stressful times we can remain healthy and cope well."

5. If your group consists of mostly or only high achievers, they may be experiencing more stress than other students in areas such as college selection and career direction. You might encourage them to try to live in the present and not be preoccupied about the future, even though there are decisions to make and applications to prepare. If they mention stress related to others' expectations, turn the discussion to the importance of doing things for themselves, not just to please others. That doesn't mean that they should automatically reject the values or wishes of their parents; they simply need to pay attention to what they are comfortable with in regard to college selection and career possibilities..

6. For closure, ask the group to comment on what was valuable about this session. As they leave, remind them to keep sorting out the sources of their stress.

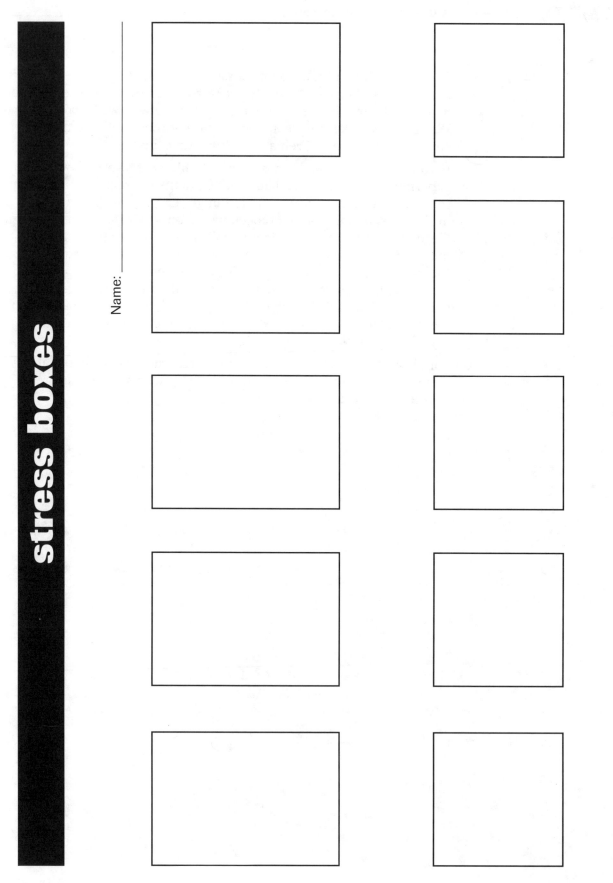

Name: _____

stress boxes

focus: stress
dealing with others' expectations

background

All students must deal with others' expectations. For students with high capability, this can be a special burden. For them, the expectations are probably higher and may be felt more intensely. Sometimes their parents are "living through them." Their teachers and peers may expect them to achieve great things. They also have high expectations for themselves.

It has been said that adolescents today cannot expect to surpass—or perhaps even meet—the level of attainment their parents have reached. This may be the first time in our history when it has not been widely accepted that every succeeding generation will go farther, do more, and have more than their parents, at least for middle and upper income levels. Certainly, many adolescents will be successful, and some will be more successful than their parents. But it can be frightening to be 15 years old (or older) with no clear vision of career direction, no idea what the future will bring (economically or in terms of job availability), and the belief that parents' success levels are unreachable. That is how many teenagers feel.

This session gives students a chance to articulate the expectations placed on them and their feelings about those expectations. They might even realize that they have higher expectations for themselves than others have for them—and that the pressure to achieve may come mostly from within.

Whatever the source, expectations can place great stress on students. It is important to bring them out into the open, and a discussion group is a good place to do this.

Ultimately, all students must ask themselves, "What do I want and need? Whose life am I trying to live? Am I too aware of what someone else wants or needs me to be?"

objectives

- Students articulate what they perceive to be others' expectations of them, and their feelings about the perceived expectations.
- They discover that their peers experience similar pressures and stressors.
- They learn that sometimes expectations are assumed and perhaps are not real.

- They learn that it is important to discuss expectations with their family and to express feelings about those expectations. Family members may not realize that they are communicating certain expectations to the student, or that their expectations are causing stress. Parents and other significant persons might welcome the chance to clarify what they do and do not expect of the student.

- Students focus on the importance of satisfying their own needs and taking care of themselves in life, rather than deferring too much to others' wishes for them.

suggestions

1. Introduce the topic with some ideas from the background information. Hand out the "Expectations" activity sheet (page 162) and allow time for the students to answer the questions. For students who do not live with or have frequent contact with one or both parents, ask them to think of other adults in their lives who have special influence on or interest in them, such as a teacher, counselor, pastor, or other adult relative.

2. Encourage the students to share their responses. Whenever necessary, ask questions or request further clarification. Or let the group perform this function.

   After each student has finished sharing, you might ask the group something like this: "Is there any potential for conflict in what he/she has just reported?" Allow time for discussion. Invite the group to contribute suggestions for avoiding or resolving the conflict. Ask, "What is the connection between conflict and stress?" Encourage students to share their own experiences with stress caused by conflicting expectations.

3. Ask, "When it comes to your life direction, who is the *most* important person to satisfy?" (Yourself.) To generate discussion on this issue, ask questions like the following.

   - What are *your* wants and needs? What might they be ten years from now? Fifteen years from now?

   - What might happen if you deny your own needs in favor of satisfying other peoples' needs? How might this affect your choices concerning college and career, where you live, who you marry, and so on?

   - (Especially for underachievers with high capability): How important is it to match intellectual level with educational level, job level, spouse, fellow workers?

   - How important is it for females to plan to be self-supporting?

   - How important is it to be flexible about future direction during the first year or two of college? (Very important, since they will be exposed to new options.)

   - How important is money to success? To satisfaction?

▶ Have you ever considered arranging a short-term internship or one-day career-shadowing experience for yourself in one or two possible career areas while you are still in high school?

▶ Do you think that people who have many talents and abilities have a particular problem with finding direction in life? Give your reasons for thinking this.

▶ Have you ever asked your parents what expectations they have for you? Do you think you are making accurate assumptions about what they expect? Who has the higher expectations for you—you yourself, or your parents?

▶ How do you plan to deal with parental expectations that conflict with yours?

▶ How could you initiate a conversation with your parents about such conflict? Why might you want to bring up the subject and discuss it with them?

4. For closure, ask the group to comment on what occurred during the session. What did they think about during the discussion? Did anything in the discussion help them to focus, give them courage, or make them feel more optimistic? Did anything discourage them? Did they find that they share concerns with others in the group? How do they feel now about paying attention to their needs and wants in regard to others' expectations? Is that being "selfish"?

expectations

Name: _____

What does your mother (or another significant adult female in your life) see you doing and being ten or fifteen years from now? _____

_____

_____

_____

_____

What does your father (or another significant adult male in your life) see you doing and being ten or fifteen years from now? _____

_____

_____

_____

_____

What do you see yourself doing and being ten or fifteen years from now?

_____

_____

_____

_____

_____

Who expects the most of you? _____

Can you identify some areas of disagreement and potential conflict? If so, what are they?

_____

_____

_____

_____

_____

role models and strategies for coping with stress

This session focuses on adult role models for coping with stress. As your group considers where we learn our coping responses—the main theme of the session—it might be helpful to offer the following thoughts about learning to cope more effectively with stress.

- We have the capability to manage stress and make situations less threatening.

- We cannot avoid all overly stressful situations, but we can learn to react in ways that do not hurt us. We can learn to problem-solve, make adjustments, and take care of ourselves.

- Learning to control our reactions to stress is the key to effective coping.

- We can pause before reacting to stressful situations and think about possible responses and consequences.

- We can respond creatively, think positively, and learn to see stressful situations as opportunities for personal growth.

- We can remember that fears of "catastrophes" in the past were often unfounded.

- Instead of running from stressful situations, we can work on ways to respond that allow us to retain control of our lives.

- We can talk about stress and responses to stress with our family, friends, teachers, coaches, or co-workers. A good listener can help us sort out our stress.

- We can learn to relax, take time to rest, exercise, eat healthfully, and cut down on caffeinated drinks. When we feel good physically, we can cope with stress more effectively.

objectives

- Students recognize that responses to stress and coping strategies are often learned from adult role models.

- They discover that it is possible to learn new responses to stress and unlearn habitual responses.

163

1. Introduce the idea that we learn how to cope with stress from significant others who model coping strategies for us. Some are better role models than others. Ask the students to list on paper the significant adults in their lives, and then briefly describe how each deals with stressful situations. Explain that these should be not only adults they like and respect, but any adult who is significant to their lives.

2. Encourage the students to share their lists and descriptions. Afterward, ask them to compare the adults' responses to stress with their own responses. Ask questions like the following.

   ▶ When you compare your responses to the adults' responses, can you draw any conclusions?

   ▶ Are your responses a lot like the responses of an adult you know? Are they just the opposite? Are they somewhere in between?

   ▶ How well do the coping strategies you use work for you? Are they effective and beneficial?

   ▶ Do you wish you could respond to stress in another way? If so, what might that be?

3. Turn the focus to some specifics of how group members respond to stress. Ask questions like the following.

   ▶ Do you feel that you cannot or should not express anger or frustration when responding to stress?

   ▶ Do you feel that you must always stay in control, be rational, and stay even-tempered for the sake of everyone else?

   ▶ What problems might be caused by stuffing or burying your feelings?

   ▶ What might happen if you responded to stress in some unexpected way?

   ▶ How much do you talk about stress with your family and friends? If you don't, is it because talking about stress is threatening to your image?

   ▶ When you feel stressed, or when you respond ineffectively to stress, do you feel as if you have "failed"?

4. Invite the students to share successful coping strategies. Ask, "What have you learned about responding to stress? What do you do to relax? How do you take care of yourself?"

5. Lead the group in a relaxation exercise, or invite someone in the school or community to visit your group for this purpose.

6. For closure, ask one or more volunteers to summarize what has been helpful in the session. If appropriate, commend the students for their honesty and thoughtfulness. Wish them "good coping" during the time until the next meeting, and encourage them to keep monitoring their own and others' responses to stress.

focus: stress

is it harder to be an adolescent today?

Is it true, as some say, that many of today's young people are spoiled by a "soft life"? Perhaps—but consider the enormous numbers who live in poverty, in blighted urban areas, in abusive and dysfunctional families. Consider, too, the changes in family structure, in geographic mobility and "roots," in the rising crime rate, in the job market, in societal and family violence, in the power of the media for influencing behavior, in the bombardment of information from many sources. Consider also the *rapidity* of change. It is possible that the youth of today are stronger and more resilient than any preceding generation because of what they must contend with and adapt to.

This session can give adolescents a chance to explore the validity of that claim of strength and resilience. Do they have more to deal with than their parents or grandparents did when they were young? Can preceding generations even begin to imagine what it is like to be a middle school/junior high or high school student in the United States today? Can teenagers apply the same strategies their parents used to survive their adolescence, or are these strategies defunct?

The discussion is not meant to promote a "poor us" attitude in a group. It can, however, be another opportunity to gain skills in articulating feelings, and for shedding new light on how young people are surviving today, regardless of whether circumstances are worse than they were in the past. Seeing themselves as strong for what they are accomplishing in stressful times might strengthen their self-esteem and help them move ahead in life more positively.

objectives

- Students are reminded that growing up today is different from growing up in their parents' or grandparents' generations.
- They learn to articulate the stresses in their lives and consider them in the context of this decade.

1. Introduce the topic by asking, "Have you ever been accused of being lazy, spoiled, taking things for granted, or having an easy life compared to when your parents or grandparents were your age?"

2. Invite the students to brainstorm some ways this decade is different from preceding decades, in regard to being an adolescent. Ask, "What makes life today easier? More difficult? Just different?"

3. Ask, "Do you think that each generation's adults look to their children to achieve what they did not? Do you feel that your parents are pushing you to do that? In what ways? In what areas of your life?" If students do not mention academics, social relationships, marriage, and career, introduce these areas into the discussion.

4. If your group is made up of students with high ability and achievement, ask questions like the following.

   ◗ Many highly successful people who have been living in the "fast lane" are downscaling to simpler lifestyles lately. How do you view this?

   ◗ How is the stress of young people today affected by the "overchoice" inherent in college selection, career options, course selection, geographical location options—even breakfast cereals and toothpaste?

   ◗ Do you have more expectations of yourself and others than your parents did?

   ◗ Compare your sense of "place" and neighborhood "roots" to your parents' at your age. Are they different?

5. If your group contains students who are at risk because of socio-economic factors, family dysfunction, substance abuse, or neglect, ask questions like the following. They are appropriate for other students as well.

   ◗ How has your life been affected by recent changes in our society? (Mention some ideas from the background information.)

   ◗ How do you feel you compare with your parents' generation in personal strength, wisdom, and the ability to deal with stress?

   ◗ Are you working hard at jobs outside of school, caring for siblings, walking a long way to school, lacking private space, distracted from concentrating on schoolwork by your environment, contributing to family income, being a "parent" to someone in your family (or to your own children), and/or responsible for food preparation for your family *and* for meeting all or most of your own personal needs?

   ◗ Are some of you dealing with disabilities or illness?

6. Invite the group to consider the social stresses of today's teenagers. Ask, "Are social stresses today different from those of 10 to 20 years ago?"

    In exploring this issue, it does not matter whether the students assess preceding generations accurately. There is value simply in expressing their feelings about their lives.

7. For closure, ask, "Did today's session cause you to think about your life in a different way? What thoughts and feelings did this discussion provoke in you?"

focus: stress
taking a load off

This session is meant to give group members a chance to talk about the safe havens in their lives—places and circumstances where they feel they can be themselves and be accepted unconditionally, where they do not feel judged or criticized, where they feel in control, comfortable, and peaceful, where they can "take a load off." This is a low-resistance topic, and even the most cynical student will probably feel free to comment.

Sharing a "no-sharp-edges" self, with no stiff defenses, in a supportive group atmosphere can contribute to an improved outlook on life. There may be individuals who do not feel they have a place where they can relax and "be themselves." Perhaps those students can feel appreciated unconditionally here.

One part of the suggested format for this session involves students' sharing places/circumstances where they feel "dumb" and where they feel "smart"—or "good" and "bad." As always, discovering what they have in common might help them feel less lonely or alienated.

objectives

- Students articulate positive feelings associated with places and circumstances where they feel very comfortable.

- They let down their defenses and pay attention to their own and others' feelings, needs, and experiences.

- They learn that everyone feels "dumb" in some environments and "smart" in others.

suggestions

NOTE: Depending on your group, it might be preferable to begin with suggestion #3 and then move to #1 and #2.

1. Have the students think of a place where they feel peaceful, centered, comfortable, and "good"—or a person who helps them feel that they can unload their burdens and relax. Encourage them to share their thoughts, giving enough details and feelings that the other group members can understand the importance of the person or place. Students might talk about home, their room, school, church or temple, teachers in general, one teacher in particular, one or both parents, a

friend or friends, one or more siblings, or a special relative, to name several possibilities.

2. If some students can think of no such place or person, ask them to describe an ideal, hoped-for, super-comfortable situation. You might also ask, "How have you learned to cope with not having such a place or person in your life?"

   If someone takes this opportunity to describe a chaotic, debilitating, or otherwise nonsupportive home environment, listen and receive the information with encouraging comments and body language. You might say something like, "That's a pretty tough situation. I admire your strength and courage in dealing with it as well as you have."

3. Ask the students to list on paper those situations where they feel "dumb" or inept. Encourage them to share with the group. Next, ask them to list on paper those situations where they feel "smart" or confident, and encourage them to share these as well.

   It is assumed that even students who do not do well in school feel "smart" in some situations—if not at school, then perhaps with their friends, at home, or in their areas of interest. Gifted students usually find this to be an interesting exercise, since it is comforting to hear that *all* experience "feeling dumb" in some situations, and that some who appear highly confident (like themselves, perhaps) are, in fact, not always at ease.

4. For closure, ask one or more volunteers to summarize the session. What were some common needs expressed? Some frequently mentioned places and situations? Did the students experience any insights about themselves?

focus: stress
procrastination

background

Procrastination! Parents and teachers of adolescents know what a problem it is. The adolescents themselves probably find it equally frustrating.

Bright students know that they can delay and delay...and then finish a project or paper at the eleventh hour. Those who don't buy into the "do-or-die" mode also procrastinate, but they may or may not deliver in the end. Students at risk may have many energy-draining things interfering with schoolwork, and they may not be able to concentrate on it, but they also might simply procrastinate—like everyone else.

Most students procrastinate at *something*—cleaning their room, doing major assignments, calling Grandma, sending a thank-you note, completing college applications, signing up for the SAT, applying for a job, turning in next year's registration form, getting their car license. Perhaps it makes little difference most of the time, but it can become a dangerous and self-destructive habit. It can cause stress and tension during the final, intense effort. It can cause both concern and frustration in those who inevitably worry about the procrastinator.

What can students do about procrastination? They can start by talking about it in a caring, supportive, understanding group that probably contains its share of procrastinators.

objectives

- Students look objectively at procrastination and how it affects them personally.
- They consider some possible causes of procrastination and ways to do something about it.

suggestions

1. Introduce the topic by asking, "Are there any procrastinators in this group?" After a certain amount of denial and possibly joking, some—or all—group members will admit to procrastinating occasionally or often. Then ask, "What kinds of things do you procrastinate about?" As they give their responses, list them on a chalkboard or a large sheet of paper.

2. Ask the group, "Does procrastination ever cause problems for you? For other people in your life? What kinds of problems?"

3. Encourage the students to consider what might contribute to their procrastination. If they need help, ask questions like the following.

   ▶ Does procrastination have a payoff that makes up for or outweighs any problems it causes? What kind of payoff?

   ▶ Does it motivate you to do other things first?

   ▶ What would you lose if you did something early?

   ▶ Do you feel that you work more efficiently when you do things at the last minute—or less efficiently?

   ▶ Do you think that procrastination is a kind of rebellion or resistance? Rebellion against what? Resistance to what?

   ▶ Do you have problems concentrating on what you need to do?

4. Help the students to identify the areas where they tend to procrastinate. Ask questions like the following.

   ▶ How many of you procrastinate only in schoolwork? Only with household chores? Only with tasks that involve planning for the future, such as college applications or course choices?

   ▶ How many of you procrastinate in almost every area of your life?

   ▶ Was there a time in the past when you didn't procrastinate?

5. Use questions like the following to help the group make the connection between procrastination and other issues.

   ▶ Do other people worry about the things you have to do—and remind you to do them?

   ▶ Have you developed a habit of waiting for others to tell you what to do and when?

   ▶ Is your procrastination part of an ongoing conflict with a parent or a sibling?

   ▶ Does passive procrastination give you a sense of power and control over certain situations or relationships?

   ▶ Is your procrastination the result of stress?

   ▶ How do you feel when you procrastinate?

6. Ask the students to consider what might happen if they suddenly stopped procrastinating and did everything early—or at least without a last-minute rush. Invite them to explore this idea by asking questions like the following.

   ▶ Who would be affected?

   ▶ How would your life change?

   ▶ What would you lose?

   ▶ What would you gain?

➤ Would you feel better or worse about yourself?

➤ Would you feel more or less stress in your life?

7. For closure, ask the group to comment on what they heard and felt during this session. Do they think that procrastination is mostly good or mostly bad? Does it serve a purpose? Is it a habit? If so, should it be changed?

focus: stress
substance abuse

background

Most students probably will have learned something about substance abuse in health classes and/or school assemblies in early adolescence. However, they may not have had the opportunity to discuss this vital subject in a group of peers led by a caring adult. This session gives students a safe place to express their feelings about substance abuse and to hear what others have to say.

important

Prior to this session, be sure to familiarize yourself with the topic through research and talking with other knowledgeable adults. You will need a reasonably good understanding of various substances and their effects in order to feel confident talking to your group—and to avoid giving them erroneous information. However, it is best if you do not present yourself as an expert (even if you are). Let the students teach *you*.

If your group has been created to deal specifically with substance abuse problems, most or all of the sessions in this book are appropriate. For this session, you may wish to gather more specific information and ideas for group content regarding substance abuse or children of alcoholics. Contact organizations that deal regularly with those issues.

You may want to consider inviting a counselor or administrator from an area substance-abuse treatment facility to visit your group during this session. You might suggest that he or she explain what treatment involves (it usually includes dealing with family issues and personal problems) and present some of the harsh realities of addiction in adolescents.

objectives

- Students learn how some of their peers feel about substance use and abuse.
- They articulate their feelings about substance use and abuse occurring in their age group.

suggestions

1. Begin by asking the group to "teach" you about substance use and abuse in their age group. What can they tell you about substances, numbers of students and substances involved, frequency of use, types or groups of students involved, parental attitudes about substance use and abuse, parties, and behavior—especially dangerous behavior—that is related to alcohol and other drug use?

   Remind the group of the need for confidentiality; some students may share sensitive information, and they should know that it will be safe to do so. Encourage them *not* to name names.

2. Ask the students, "How do you feel about the information you have just shared?" After hearing their feelings, continue the discussion with questions like the following.

   ▶ Do you feel pressured to use drugs or alcohol?

   ▶ Do you feel like an outsider if you are not into drugs or alcohol?

   ▶ Without naming names, do you know peers whose substance abuse is interfering with schoolwork and other aspects of their life?

   ▶ Do you know of anyone who has died, or almost died, from drug or alcohol abuse?

   ▶ Do you know anyone who has been in treatment for substance abuse?

   ▶ Are all adolescents vulnerable to becoming involved with alcohol and other drugs?

   ▶ What motivates someone to use alcohol or other drugs?

   ▶ Is it possible that adolescents who use drugs and alcohol are attempting to gain control over their lives?

   ▶ Are feelings of insecurity related to why teenagers abuse substances?

3. Instruct the students to consider how their families view the use of drugs and alcohol. Ask questions like the following—but be aware that you might not get any response.

   ▶ Does your family disapprove of other drugs but approve of or tolerate alcohol? How do you feel about that?

   ▶ What do you know about alcoholism?

4. Ask, "What are your personal 'rules' regarding alcohol and other drugs? Do you make a distinction between alcohol and other drugs? Should you?"

5. For closure, ask a volunteer to summarize the discussion, with special emphasis on the information shared in suggestion #1. Express your hope that the students will make wise choices with regard to substance use.

focus: stress

vulnerability to cults and demagogues

background

Under certain personal circumstances, almost anyone can become vulnerable to the influence of cults and demagogues. However, it appears that people of high capability may be particularly vulnerable. Their talent, intelligence, and idealism are not always enough to protect them from the appeal of groups that promise comfort, caring, and security in a world that seems uncertain and confusing. Perhaps they are vulnerable because their hypersensitive minds tire of all the options and possibilities and are eager for "an answer." They are sometimes innocent and naive, might be lonely and insecure, often have problems regarding identity, and have concerns about "meaning" and "purpose."

For people in transition—beginning college, emerging from depression, experiencing personal problems—cults *appear* to offer enticing possibilities:

- an appealing message of simplicity and perfection
- unconditional acceptance and love
- structure and purpose
- ready answers to complex questions and relief from tough decisions
- something to "do" regarding religion, something many denominational churches do not offer
- a promise to fill the personal "emptiness"
- something new and different
- a "caring group."

Joining a cult often means separating from one's family of origin. Disorientation leaves new recruits vulnerable to mind control. Many cults claim religious underpinnings, but all have human leaders, who often draw the group tightly around themselves and take advantage of their disorientation and isolation.

objectives

- Students gain understanding about what is involved in cult activity.
- They think about their own vulnerability to cult involvement.

suggestions

1. Begin by asking the students what they already know about cults. In addition to what they offer, share parts of the background information and other information you may have gathered about cults in preparing for this session. You may want to read aloud the following paragraph from *The Wrong Way Home* by Arthur J. Deikman (Boston: Beacon Press, 1990):

   "Usually, the word *cult* refers to a group led by a charismatic leader who has spiritual, therapeutic, or messianic pretensions, and indoctrinates the members with his or her idiosyncratic beliefs. Typically, members are dependent on the group for their emotional and financial needs and have broken off ties with those outside. The more complete the dependency and the more rigid the barriers separating members from non-believers, the more danger the cult will exploit and harm its members."

   Deikman believes that the wish for a powerful, protective parent can cause people of any age and position, even those not in cults, to look to a strong leader for guidance and willingly give away autonomy in exchange for freedom from tough decisions, complex thinking, and uncertainty.

2. Encourage the students to discuss their own vulnerabilities. Ask questions like the following.

   ‣ Do you sometimes feel worn down by complexity, decision-making, family problems, questions about religion, perplexity about "meaning," loneliness, and frustration with an imperfect world?

   ‣ Do you ever dream of giving yourself over to someone who can take care of you, answer all of your questions, protect you from the world, and tell you what to think?

   ‣ At what times, and in what circumstances, have you been vulnerable to the wish to turn all thinking over to someone else?

   Reassure the group that these feelings and dreams are normal and very human. However, they need to be aware of their own vulnerability when cult recruiters come calling—perhaps during midterms during their first year of college, or when they have just broken up with a boyfriend or girlfriend, or when they are otherwise in a weakened emotional condition.

3. For closure, ask volunteers to share feelings and thoughts they had during this discussion. Encourage them to keep taking responsibility for their own lives—and to keep thinking for themselves, even when they are weary and exhausted.

focus: stress
centering

background

In our fragmented, conflict-ridden world, it is important to stop frenetic behavior, tune in to the self, plant feet solidly on the ground, relax, and feel affirmed. This session gives you the opportunity to teach students one way to do this: by "centering" themselves through a relaxation exercise. Explain that while you will be leading the exercise in group, this is something they can do for themselves whenever they feel the need to slow down and calm down.

objectives

- Students are reminded that they often take their bodies for granted.
- During a leader-directed relaxation exercise, they focus on their bodies. They relax and "center" themselves.

suggestions

1. Introduce the topic by asking, "Do you sometimes think that you take your body for granted?" If some or all group members reply in the affirmative, ask, "How much do you pay attention to fitness? Nutrition? Getting enough rest? Eating regular meals? Your posture? The physical effects of stress? How much do you feel that you take care of your body? How well do you eat? How regular is your sleep?" They might share anecdotes about times when they were reminded to pay attention to their bodies, such as during illness, after an accident, or when excessively fatigued.

2. Say, "Now we're going to try something a little different. We're going to relax together, as a group, and think about ourselves physically." Students should be sitting squarely on comfortable chairs, since it is best if they do not have to move once the exercise begins. Slouching, crossed legs, leaning on a table—these and other "unsolid" postures work less well than sitting upright with both feet on the floor.

   When everyone seems ready, read the following *very slowly* in a well-modulated voice:

   "Close your eyes and just relax . . . . Now move your lower back so that it touches the back of your chair squarely . . . . Wiggle your toes and then set your feet solidly on the floor . . . . Touch your thumbs to your fingertips several times and feel those extremities . . . . Now sit very quietly and think about your body . . . your physical space . . . your limits . . . . Mentally trace the outline of your body . . . . Relax and let your body occupy your space comfortably . . . . Mentally, without moving, check to see if you are relaxed . . . . Concentrate on your thighs . . . your arms . . . your hands . . . your shoulders . . . your face . . . your eyes . . . your jaw . . . your mouth . . . . Are they relaxed? . . . Let them be slack . . . . Un-tense all of your muscles . . . . Now I'm going to be silent for one whole minute while you tune in to your breathing. If you think about other things, it's okay. If your mind wanders, gently bring it back. Then tune in to your relaxed body, breathing . . . . Recheck one part of your body at a time . . . your thighs . . . your arms . . . your hands . . . your jaw . . . your eyes . . . . If you realize you're thinking about other things, come back . . . . Check your body again . . . Tune in to it . . . . Now I'll be silent . . . ."

Wait one minute before continuing.

"Does your body feel good? . . . Feel yourself at the center of your body, at the center of yourself . . . . How have you been doing lately? . . . Are you taking care of yourself? . . . Your feet are on the ground . . . . You are unique and strong . . . . You have your own story . . . . You're okay . . . .

"Now sit quietly for one more minute with your eyes still closed. Check out your body. It might be quite relaxed. Your breathing may be very quiet. I will tell you when it is time."

Wait one minute before continuing.

"Now slowly open your eyes . . . . Take a deep breath without moving your body . . . . Your fingertips may tingle a bit . . . . How do you feel? . . . You can slowly begin to move now."

3. Encourage the group to talk about the relaxation experience. Were they comfortable? Did they relax? Were they distracted? How do they feel?

4. Tell them that such a relaxation exercise, even for 5 or 10 minutes, can help them before a performance, before a test, if they are too tired to read an assignment, and even to start their day if they haven't slept well. They may be less groggy afterward than if they took a nap instead. Some people relax in such a way daily, maybe more than once.

5. For closure, thank the students for their cooperation, if appropriate. Wish them a good day and a good week. Encourage them to take care of themselves.

index

a

Ability tests, 53–54
Acceptance, 168–169
Activity sheets
  generally, 5
  for learning styles, 50
  for uniquenesses and similarities, 126
Adderholdt-Elliott, Miriam, 41
An Adult's Guide to Style (Gregorc), 48
Advice, 134–135
Affective needs, iv, 2, 8
Alcohol. *See* Substance abuse
Alone time, 109–110
Anger, permission for, 64
Asking for help, 136–137
Assessment, 100–102
  of group discussion, 18, 21–23
  and others' perceptions (form), 119
  of self (form), 102
  of values (form), 105–106
Assumptions, 3
At-risk students. *See* Students at risk
Athletes, sessions for, 12
Authority
  form, 128, 130–131
  responding to, 127–131
Award application forms, and personal strengths, 30

b

Butler, Kathleen, 48

c

Career choice, and knowing self, 27
Centering, 177–178
Change, 165–167
Choice, freedom of, (form), 97
Classroom, discussions in, 12
Closure, suggestions for, 5, 16
Communication skills, 2
Compassion, 145–148. *See also* Tolerance
Compliments, giving and receiving, 121–122
Compulsivity, 44–46
Confidence. *See* Self-esteem

Control, 72–73
Counseling
  defined, 7
  of individual group members, 11
  for underachievement, 57
  See also Guided discussion groups
Courage, 90–92
Cults
  defined, 176
  vulnerability to, 175–176

d

Daydreaming, 98–99
Decision-making, 2
Deikman, Arthur J., on cults, 176
Demagogues, vulnerability to, 175–176
Depression, 2
  sessions for, 5
  and underachievement, 57
Discipline, and learning style, 47. *See also* Authority
Discouragement, 120–122. *See also* Encouragement
Discussion groups. *See* Guided discussion groups
Disliked self. *See* Identity
Drug use. *See* Substance abuse

e

Emotional bombshells, handling, 11–12
Encouragement, 120–122. *See also* Discouragement
Endings. *See* Closure
Environment, and learning style, 47
Esteem. *See* Self-esteem
Ethics, of leaders, 10
Evaluation. *See under* Guided discussion groups
Expectations
  form, 162
  and perfectionism, 40
Extremes, 38–39
Extroverts, 38, 109

f

Facade, 33–35
  of adults, 35

vs. real self, 33, 34
  See also Image
Failure, 107–108
Feedback, student, 2, 28
Feelings, articulating, 27, 28, 33
Frames of Mind (Gardner), 55
Freedom, 95–97
  of choice (form), 97
Friendship, and talking about self, 27
Fun, having, 83–85
  and adults, 85
  and being childlike, 84
  creative, 84

g

Gardner, Howard, 55–56
Gender
  and group composition, 6–7
  and test scores, 55
Giants in the Earth (Rolvaag), 93
Gifted students
  defining, 51, 53
  and grades, 51, 53
  and group composition, 6
  and intensity, 44
  and perfectionism, 40
  response by to groups, 1
  sessions for, 4, 6, 166
  and underachievement, 57–58
  working with, 2
Giftedness, Conflict, and Underachievement (Whitmore), 58
Gifts, we would like. *See* Needs and wants
Giving, 132–133
Grades, and defining self, 53–56
Gregorc, Anthony, 48
The Gregorc Style Delineator (Gregorc), 48
Groups, discussion. *See* Guided discussion groups
Guided discussion groups, 1–3, 6–8, 12
  for articulating thoughts and feelings, 27, 28, 33
  assumptions to keep in mind, 3
  benefits of, 1
  composition of, 6–7

discovering similarities in, 33
evaluation of (form), 21–23
follow-up (form), 20
forming, 6–8
generally, 1–3
getting started, 14–16
guidelines, 18
motives for establishing, 8
permission for student
  participation (form), 17
preventive function of, 1
purpose of, 2–3, 18
sessions, 3–6
  background information for, 5
  closure of, 5, 16
  cohesiveness of, 12
  focus of, 4, 9
  general description of, 3–4
  objectives for, 4
  for special populations, 5–6
  suggestions for, 4
sharing doubts in, 33
size of, 6
starting, 14–16
uses for, 12
warm-up (form), 19
See also Leaders of groups

h

Haan, Norma McLane, iv
Hate groups, 145
Heacox, Diane, 58
Help. See Asking for help; Safe
  havens
Heroes/heroines, 81–82
Hunking, Loila, iv
Hypocrisy
  dealing with, 2
  facade as, 33

i

Ideal self. See Identity
Identity
  assessing three selves (form), 32
  and defining self, 51–52, 53–56
  developing personal, 27–28, 74
  and facade, 33–35
  and personal symbol, 111
  of three selves, 31–32
  See also Self-esteem
Image, 93–94. See also Facade;
  Identity
Influences, 123–124
Intelligence
  multiple, 55–56
  and test scores, 55

Intensity, 44–46
Introspection, 3
Introverts, 38, 109
It's All in Your Mind (Butler), 48

j

Job interviews, and personal
  strengths, 30
Jones, Ruth, iv
Journal-writing, 10–11
  as response to literature, 1

k

Kiersey, D., 109

l

Lauer, Jack, iv
Leaders of groups
  assessing readiness, 8–9
  ethical behavior as, 10
  guidelines for, 9–12
  tips for, 15–16
Leaning on others. See Asking for
  help
Learning styles, 47–50
  activity sheet, 50
  of groups, 49
Limitations, 29–30
Listening
  need for, 2
  and nonverbal behavior, 16
  skills, 3
  to students, 3
Loneliness, 109–110

m

Messages, and defining self, 51–52
Mireley, M., 58
Mistakes, making, 79–80
  permission for, 64
Moderation, 44–46

n

Names, 67–68
  importance of, 67
  nicknames, 67
Needs and wants, 138–140, 141–144
  forms, 140, 144
  getting them met, 141–144

o

Oldfather, Penny, iv
Ostrander, Joan, iv
Others, and self, 113–148
  assessing (form), 119

background generally, 115
objectives of sessions on, 116
See also Perceptions

p

Parents, 13
"Patterns of underachievement
  among gifted students" (Richert), 58
Perceptions
  form, 119
  by others, 3, 117–119
Perfectionism, 40–43
  breaking cycle of, 40, 43
  good/bad aspects of, 41
  and self-worth, 42
  and success, 107
Perfectionism (Adderholdt-Elliott), 41
Permission, 63–66
  giving self (form), 66
  and intelligence, 63
Personal history. See Story, personal
Personal symbol, 111
Personality types, 38, 109
Phonies. See Facade
Please Understand Me
  (Kiersey/Bates), 109
Priorities, 69–71
Problem-solving, 1, 2
Process, vs. product, iv, 3
Procrastination, 170–172

r

Real self. See Identity
Resilience, 165
Richert, E.S., 58
Rimm, Sylvia, 58
Risk-taking, and perfectionism, 40
Role models
  and authority, 127
  for coping with stress, 163–164
  group leaders as, 9, 15
Rolvaag, O.E., 93

s

Safe havens, 168–169
Scholarship application forms, and
  personal strengths, 30
Self
  in general, 27–28
  See also Identity; Others
Self-assessment. See Assessment
Self-awareness, and self-assessment,
  100
Self-esteem, 3, 74–78
  improving, 1

and performance, 42
rating (form), 78
and strengths, 29–30, 165
Selfishness, permission for, 64
Sessions. *See under* Guided
  discussion groups
Shame
  and being childlike, 35
  and limitations, 29
Shyness
  as positive trait, 38
  of students, 3, 6, 11
  See also Introverts
Similarities, 125–126
  activity sheet, 126
Smoking. *See* Substance abuse
Social skills, 2, 3
Special populations, sessions for,
  4, 5–6. *See also* Gifted students;
  Students at risk
Standardized achievement tests,
  54–55, 56
Stephens, Fred, iv
Stereotypes, 36–37, 58
Story, personal, 86–89
  form, 88–89
Strength, 29–30, 165
Stress, 149–178
  as assumption, 3
  background generally, 151–152
  boxes (form), 155–156, 158
  coping with, 2, 151, 163–164
  defining, 153–154
  lowering levels of, 1
  objectives of sessions on, 152
  physical responses to, 153–154

sessions for, 5, 152
social, 167
sources of, 155–158
synonyms for, 153
Student participation, 7, 17. *See also*
  Gifted students; Students at risk
Students at risk
  approaching, 7–8
  asking for help, 136
  sessions for, 4, 5, 166
Substance abuse, 173–174
Success, 107–108
Support
  groups, 2, 7
  of others, iv
Systems theory, iv

t

Taking stock. *See* Assessment
Teaching style, and learning style, 47
Test scores, and defining self, 53–56
Thoughts, articulating, 27, 28, 33
Three selves. *See under* Identity
Time, 69–71
  healing effect of, 3
  making better use of, 1, 70
  managing (form), 71
Tobacco. *See* Substance abuse
Tolerance, 145–148. *See also*
  Compassion
Topics
  not covered, 2
  secret, 12
Traits, extreme, 38–39
Trust, establishing, 3

u

Underachievement, 57–62
  causes of, 57, 59
  counseling for, 57
  defining, 51, 53
  and depression, 57
  form, 62
  and grades, 51, 53
  as habit, 57
  sessions for, 6
Underachievement Syndrome
  (Rimm), 58
Understanding the Gifted Adolescent
  (Mireley/Genshaft), 58
Uniqueness, 125–126
  activity sheet, 126
Up From Underachievement
  (Heacox), 58

v

Values, 103–106
  assessing (form), 105–106
Vulnerability, 175–176

w

Weaknesses. *See* Limitations
Whitmore, Joanne, 58
Widman, Gail, iv
The Wrong Way Home
  (Deikman), 176

about the author

Jean Sunde Peterson, M.A.T., M.A., taught for twenty-four years in Iowa, Minnesota, South Dakota, and Berlin, Germany, before coming to the University of Iowa in 1990 for doctoral work in counseling. For the past several years she has conducted workshops and consulted with schools about programming for the gifted, social and emotional needs of the gifted, group counseling, multicultural concerns, and underachievement. She was an adjunct faculty member for many years at Augustana College, Sioux Falls, South Dakota, in English and foreign-language teaching methodology, and created summer language camps for children there. She has authored several small textbooks and teaching guides and approximately 20 articles and chapters dealing with English, foreign languages, and education of the gifted. She is also the author of a collection of poems, *Gifted At Risk*. A former South Dakota Teacher of the Year, Jean is featured in "Profiles in Successful Practice" in *Educational Psychology and Classroom Practice* (Allyn & Bacon, 1992). She developed discussion groups for adolescents in Sioux Falls and in Iowa City, Iowa.

MORE FREE SPIRIT BOOKS

Bringing Up Parents:
The Teenager's Handbook
by Alex J. Packer, Ph.D.

Straight talk and specific suggestions on how teens can take the initiative to resolve conflicts with parents, improve family relationships, earn trust, accept responsibility, and help create a healthier, happier home environment. Ages 13 and up.

272 pp; illus; s/c; 7 1/4" x 9 1/4"; $14.95
ISBN: 0-915793-48-2

Fighting Invisible Tigers:
A Stress Management Guide for Teens – Revised Edition
by Earl Hipp

Advice for young people who feel frustrated, overwhelmed, or depressed about life and want to do something about it. Ages 11–18.

160 pp; s/c; 6" x 9"; $10.95
ISBN 0-915793-80-6

Also available:
A Leader's Guide to Fighting Invisible Tigers:
12 Sessions on Stress Management and Lifeskills Development
by Connie C. Schmitz, Ph.D., with Earl Hipp

136 pp; s/c; 8 1/2" x 11"; $19.95
ISBN 0-915793-81-4

Girls and Young Women Leading the Way:
20 True Stories about Leadership
by Frances A. Karnes, Ph.D., and Suzanne M. Bean, Ph.D.

These inspiring stories from girls and young women ages 8 to 21 prove that leadership is for everyone, that leadership opportunities are everywhere, and that leadership has many faces and takes many forms. Ages 11 and up.

168 pp; s/c; 6" x 9"; $11.95
ISBN 0-915793-52-0

A Gebra Named Al
by Wendy Isdell

A witty, intelligent story that blends fantasy and adventure with basic principles of mathematics and chemistry. Ages 11 and up.

128 pp; s/c; 5 1/8" x 7 1/2"; $4.95
ISBN 0-915793-58-X

Also available:
Using A Gebra Named Al in the Classroom
by Wendy Isdell

32 pp; s/c; 8 1/2" x 11"; $6.95
ISBN 0-915793-59-8

The Survival Guide for Teenagers with LD*
**(Learning Differences)*
by Rhoda Cummings, Ed.D., and Gary Fisher, Ph.D.

Advice, information, and resources to help teenagers with LD succeed at school and prepare for life as adults. Ages 13 and up; reading level Grade 6, 2nd month.

200 pp; s/c; 6" x 9"; $11.95
ISBN 0-915793-51-2

Also available:
The Survival Guide for Teenagers with LD Audio Cassettes

222 minutes on 2 cassettes
Cassettes only: $19.95; ISBN 0-915793-56-3
Book with cassettes: $28.90; ISBN 0-915793-57-1

The First Honest Book About Lies
by Jonni Kincher

Discusses the nature of lies and how we live with them every day: at home, at school, in our relationships, and in our culture. Helps kids search for truth, become active, intelligent questioners, and explore their own feelings about lies. Ages 13 and up.

176 pp; s/c; illus; 8" x 10"; $12.95
ISBN: 0-915793-43-1

Find these books in your favorite bookstore, or write or call:

Free Spirit Publishing Inc.
400 First Avenue North, Suite 616
Minneapolis, MN 55401-1730
Toll-free (800) 735-7323, Local (612) 338-2068
Fax (612) 337-5050
E-mail Help4kids@freespirit.com